PERICLES

744

PERICLES

Perry Scott King

CHELSEA HOUSE PUBLISHERS
NEW YORK
NEW HAVEN   PHILADELPHIA

EDITOR-IN-CHIEF: Nancy Toff
EXECUTIVE EDITOR: Remmel T. Nunn
MANAGING EDITOR: Karyn Gullen Browne
COPY CHIEF: Juliann Barbato
PICTURE EDITOR: Adrian G. Allen
ART DIRECTOR: Giannella Garrett
MANUFACTURING MANAGER: Gerald Levine

Staff for PERICLES:

SENIOR EDITOR: John W. Selfridge
ASSISTANT EDITORS: Sean Dolan, Kathleen McDermott
EDITORIAL ASSISTANT: Scott Ash
COPY EDITOR: Terrance Dolan
ASSOCIATE PICTURE EDITOR: Juliette Dickstein
PICTURE RESEARCHER: Karen Herman
SENIOR DESIGNER: Ghila Krajzman
ASSISTANT DESIGNER: Jill Goldreyer
PRODUCTION COORDINATOR: Joe Romano
COVER ILLUSTRATION: © Michael Garland

CREATIVE DIRECTOR: Harold Steinberg

Frontispiece courtesy of Art Resource

3 5 7 9 8 6 4 2

Library of Congress Cataloging in Publication Data

King, Perry Scott. PERICLES

(World leaders past & present)
Bibliography: p.
Includes index.
1. Pericles, 499–429 B.C.—Juvenile literature. 2. Greece—
History—Athenian supremacy, 479–431 B.C.—Juvenile
literature. 3. Statesmen—Greece—Athens—Biography—
Juvenile literature. 4. Orators—Greece—Athens—
Biography—Juvenile literature. 5. Athens (Greece)—
History—Juvenile literature. [1. Pericles, 499–429 B.C.
2. Statesmen. 3. Greece—History—Athenian supremacy,
479–431 B.C.] I. Title. II. Series.
DF228.P4K56   1988   938'.04'0924 [B] [92] 87-14621

ISBN 0-87754-547-2

Contents

CHELSEA HOUSE PUBLISHERS

WORLD LEADERS PAST & PRESENT

ADENAUER
ALEXANDER THE GREAT
MARC ANTONY
KING ARTHUR
ATATÜRK
ATTLEE
BEGIN
BEN-GURION
BISMARCK
LÉON BLUM
BOLÍVAR
CESARE BORGIA
BRANDT
BREZHNEV
CAESAR
CALVIN
CASTRO
CATHERINE THE GREAT
CHARLEMAGNE
CHIANG KAI-SHEK
CHURCHILL
CLEMENCEAU
CLEOPATRA
CORTÉS
CROMWELL
DANTON
DE GAULLE
DE VALERA
DISRAELI
EISENHOWER
ELEANOR OF AQUITAINE
QUEEN ELIZABETH I
FERDINAND AND ISABELLA
FRANCO

FREDERICK THE GREAT
INDIRA GANDHI
MOHANDAS GANDHI
GARIBALDI
GENGHIS KHAN
GLADSTONE
GORBACHEV
HAMMARSKJÖLD
HENRY VIII
HENRY OF NAVARRE
HINDENBURG
HITLER
HO CHI MINH
HUSSEIN
IVAN THE TERRIBLE
ANDREW JACKSON
JEFFERSON
JOAN OF ARC
POPE JOHN XXIII
LYNDON JOHNSON
JUÁREZ
JOHN F. KENNEDY
KENYATTA
KHOMEINI
KHRUSHCHEV
MARTIN LUTHER KING, JR.
KISSINGER
LENIN
LINCOLN
LLOYD GEORGE
LOUIS XIV
LUTHER
JUDAS MACCABEUS
MAO ZEDONG

MARY, QUEEN OF SCOTS
GOLDA MEIR
METTERNICH
MUSSOLINI
NAPOLEON
NASSER
NEHRU
NERO
NICHOLAS II
NIXON
NKRUMAH
PERICLES
PERÓN
QADDAFI
ROBESPIERRE
ELEANOR ROOSEVELT
FRANKLIN D. ROOSEVELT
THEODORE ROOSEVELT
SADAT
STALIN
SUN YAT-SEN
TAMERLANE
THATCHER
TITO
TROTSKY
TRUDEAU
TRUMAN
VICTORIA
WASHINGTON
WEIZMANN
WOODROW WILSON
XERXES
ZHOU ENLAI

ON LEADERSHIP
Arthur M. Schlesinger, jr.

LEADERSHIP, it may be said, is really what makes the world go round. Love no doubt smooths the passage; but love is a private transaction between consenting adults. Leadership is a public transaction with history. The idea of leadership affirms the capacity of individuals to move, inspire, and mobilize masses of people so that they act together in pursuit of an end. Sometimes leadership serves good purposes, sometimes bad; but whether the end is benign or evil, great leaders are those men and women who leave their personal stamp on history.

Now, the very concept of leadership implies the proposition that individuals can make a difference. This proposition has never been universally accepted. From classical times to the present day, eminent thinkers have regarded individuals as no more than the agents and pawns of larger forces, whether the gods and goddesses of the ancient world or, in the modern era, race, class, nation, the dialectic, the will of the people, the spirit of the times, history itself. Against such forces, the individual dwindles into insignificance.

So contends the thesis of historical determinism. Tolstoy's great novel *War and Peace* offers a famous statement of the case. Why, Tolstoy asked, did millions of men in the Napoleonic wars, denying their human feelings and their common sense, move back and forth across Europe slaughtering their fellows? "The war," Tolstoy answered, "was bound to happen simply because it was bound to happen." All prior history predetermined it. As for leaders, they, Tolstoy said, "are but the labels that serve to give a name to an end and, like labels, they have the least possible connection with the event." The greater the leader, "the more conspicuous the inevitability and the predestination of every act he commits." The leader, said Tolstoy, is "the slave of history."

Determinism takes many forms. Marxism is the determinism of class. Nazism the determinism of race. But the idea of men and women as the slaves of history runs athwart the deepest human instincts. Rigid determinism abolishes the idea of human freedom—

the assumption of free choice that underlies every move we make, every word we speak, every thought we think. It abolishes the idea of human responsibility, since it is manifestly unfair to reward or punish people for actions that are by definition beyond their control. No one can live consistently by any deterministic creed. The Marxist states prove this themselves by their extreme susceptibility to the cult of leadership.

More than that, history refutes the idea that individuals make no difference. In December 1931 a British politician crossing Park Avenue in New York City between 76th and 77th Streets around 10:30 P.M. looked in the wrong direction and was knocked down by an automobile—a moment, he later recalled, of a man aghast, a world aglare: "I do not understand why I was not broken like an eggshell or squashed like a gooseberry." Fourteen months later an American politician, sitting in an open car in Miami, Florida, was fired on by an assassin; the man beside him was hit. Those who believe that individuals make no difference to history might well ponder whether the next two decades would have been the same had Mario Constasino's car killed Winston Churchill in 1931 and Giuseppe Zangara's bullet killed Franklin Roosevelt in 1933. Suppose, in addition, that Adolf Hitler had been killed in the street fighting during the Munich *Putsch* of 1923 and that Lenin had died of typhus during World War I. What would the 20th century be like now?

For better or for worse, individuals do make a difference. "The notion that a people can run itself and its affairs anonymously," wrote the philosopher William James, "is now well known to be the silliest of absurdities. Mankind does nothing save through initiatives on the part of inventors, great or small, and imitation by the rest of us—these are the sole factors in human progress. Individuals of genius show the way, and set the patterns, which common people then adopt and follow."

Leadership, James suggests, means leadership in thought as well as in action. In the long run, leaders in thought may well make the greater difference to the world. But, as Woodrow Wilson once said, "Those only are leaders of men, in the general eye, who lead in action. . . . It is at their hands that new thought gets its translation into the crude language of deeds." Leaders in thought often invent in solitude and obscurity, leaving to later generations the tasks of imitation. Leaders in action—the leaders portrayed in this series—have to be effective in their own time.

And they cannot be effective by themselves. They must act in response to the rhythms of their age. Their genius must be adapted, in a phrase of William James's, "to the receptivities of the moment." Leaders are useless without followers. "There goes the mob," said the French politician hearing a clamor in the streets. "I am their leader. I must follow them." Great leaders turn the inchoate emotions of the mob to purposes of their own. They seize on the opportunities of their time, the hopes, fears, frustrations, crises, potentialities. They succeed when events have prepared the way for them, when the community is awaiting to be aroused, when they can provide the clarifying and organizing ideas. Leadership ignites the circuit between the individual and the mass and thereby alters history.

It may alter history for better or for worse. Leaders have been responsible for the most extravagant follies and most monstrous crimes that have beset suffering humanity. They have also been vital in such gains as humanity has made in individual freedom, religious and racial tolerance, social justice and respect for human rights.

There is no sure way to tell in advance who is going to lead for good and who for evil. But a glance at the gallery of men and women in *World Leaders—Past and Present* suggests some useful tests.

One test is this: do leaders lead by force or by persuasion? By command or by consent? Through most of history leadership was exercised by the divine right of authority. The duty of followers was to defer and to obey. "Theirs not to reason why,/ Theirs but to do and die." On occasion, as with the so-called "enlightened despots" of the 18th century in Europe, absolutist leadership was animated by humane purposes. More often, absolutism nourished the passion for domination, land, gold and conquest and resulted in tyranny.

The great revolution of modern times has been the revolution of equality. The idea that all people should be equal in their legal condition has undermined the old structure of authority, hierarchy and deference. The revolution of equality has had two contrary effects on the nature of leadership. For equality, as Alexis de Tocqueville pointed out in his great study *Democracy in America*, might mean equality in servitude as well as equality in freedom.

"I know of only two methods of establishing equality in the political world," Tocqueville wrote. "Rights must be given to every citizen, or none at all to anyone . . . save one, who is the master of all." There was no middle ground "between the sovereignty of all and the absolute power of one man." In his astonishing prediction of 20th-century totalitarian dictatorship, Tocqueville explained how the revolution of equality could lead to the *"Führerprinzip"* and more terrible absolutism than the world had ever known.

But when rights are given to every citizen and the sovereignty of all is established, the problem of leadership takes a new form, becomes more exacting than ever before. It is easy to issue commands and enforce them by the rope and the stake, the concentration camp and the *gulag.* It is much harder to use argument and achievement to overcome opposition and win consent. The Founding Fathers of the United States understood the difficulty. They believed that history had given them the opportunity to decide, as Alexander Hamilton wrote in the first Federalist Paper, whether men are indeed capable of basing government on "reflection and choice, or whether they are forever destined to depend . . . on accident and force."

Government by reflection and choice called for a new style of leadership and a new quality of followership. It required leaders to be responsive to popular concerns, and it required followers to be active and informed participants in the process. Democracy does not eliminate emotion from politics; sometimes it fosters demagoguery; but it is confident that, as the greatest of democratic leaders put it, you cannot fool all of the people all of the time. It measures leadership by results and retires those who overreach or falter or fail.

It is true that in the long run despots are measured by results too. But they can postpone the day of judgment, sometimes indefinitely, and in the meantime they can do infinite harm. It is also true that democracy is no guarantee of virtue and intelligence in government, for the voice of the people is not necessarily the voice of God. But democracy, by assuring the right of opposition, offers built-in resistance to the evils inherent in absolutism. As the theologian Reinhold Niebuhr summed it up, "Man's capacity for justice makes democracy possible, but man's inclination to injustice makes democracy necessary."

A second test for leadership is the end for which power is sought. When leaders have as their goal the supremacy of a master race or the promotion of totalitarian revolution or the acquisition and exploitation of colonies or the protection of greed and privilege or the preservation of personal power, it is likely that their leadership will do little to advance the cause of humanity. When their goal is the abolition of slavery, the liberation of women, the enlargement of opportunity for the poor and powerless, the extension of equal rights to racial minorities, the defense of the freedoms of expression and opposition, it is likely that their leadership will increase the sum of human liberty and welfare.

Leaders have done great harm to the world. They have also conferred great benefits. You will find both sorts in this series. Even "good" leaders must be regarded with a certain wariness. Leaders are not demigods; they put on their trousers one leg after another just like ordinary mortals. No leader is infallible, and every leader needs to be reminded of this at regular intervals. Irreverence irritates leaders but is their salvation. Unquestioning submission corrupts leaders and demands followers. Making a cult of a leader is always a mistake. Fortunately hero worship generates its own antidote. "Every hero," said Emerson, "becomes a bore at last."

The signal benefit the great leaders confer is to embolden the rest of us to live according to our own best selves, to be active, insistent, and resolute in affirming our own sense of things. For great leaders attest to the reality of human freedom against the supposed inevitabilities of history. And they attest to the wisdom and power that may lie within the most unlikely of us, which is why Abraham Lincoln remains the supreme example of great leadership. A great leader, said Emerson, exhibits new possibilities to all humanity. "We feed on genius. . . . Great men exist that there may be greater men."

Great leaders, in short, justify themselves by emancipating and empowering their followers. So humanity struggles to master its destiny, remembering with Alexis de Tocqueville: "It is true that around every man a fatal circle is traced beyond which he cannot pass; but within the wide verge of that circle he is powerful and free; as it is with man, so with communities."

1

The Funeral Oration

The first year of the Peloponnesian War had ended; the time for honoring the dead had come. On an open ground in the Greek city of Athens, a huge tent had been raised: under it lay the remains of the men who had fallen while fighting in the service of their mighty city and its empire. For two days the relatives and friends of the dead had streamed into the tent, bearing wreaths and perfumed offerings in memory of the men who had raised their spears against the enemy Sparta—the other great power in ancient Greece some four centuries before the birth of Christ.

On this the public funeral day, 10 large cypress-wood coffins—one for each of the 10 tribes of Athens—were brought into the tent. Reverently, the ceremonial attendants placed each man's bones in the coffin of his tribe. An 11th coffin stood apart from the others, empty, in silent tribute to the brave soldiers whose bodies had not been recovered.

When the attendants finished their sad task, they carried the coffins outside to wagons, where throngs of people waited to accompany the dead to

No man has ever praised those who have died for their country more eloquently than Pericles, and yet it should be remembered that what he chiefly valued was the living.
—REX WARNER
British historian

A commemorative relief from the time of the Peloponnesian War evokes sensations of melancholy and emptiness. The war between Sparta and Athens threatened to extinguish the bright achievements made by Athens during the Golden Age of classical Greece, also known as the Age of Pericles.

Pericles delivered his famous funeral oration in 431 B.C. He reinspired his fellow citizens with his belief in the prosperous and cultured democracy of Athens for which many soldiers had sacrificed their lives.

their final resting places. As the mourners followed the wagons slowly down the road to the west, loud wails arose from bereaved wives, mothers, and daughters. The moaning cries of lament continued as the wagons halted outside the city walls and the coffins were lowered into freshly dug graves.

When the last spadeful of dirt was in place, the assembled men and women turned their heads toward a man moving slowly toward a podium. Public funerals always ended with a eulogy, or funeral oration, delivered by a man chosen by the citizens. This year had been an especially momentous one for Athens, and the people had chosen as speaker the man whose voice had held greatest sway in the city's councils for much of the last three decades: Pericles. Now past 60, he walked with a steady, dignified stride, head bowed, thinking about his city, the war, and the words he must say to the people of Athens.

From the podium Pericles looked out at the expectant crowd, his eyes coming to rest on four people standing close together. One was a brawny sailor who pulled one of many oars on a massive warship, part of the navy that guarded Athens's sea empire. Behind the mariner was a sour-faced aristocrat whose large tract of land near Mount Parnes to the north had been ravaged that summer by the enemy army. Next to the landholder stood the owner of a masonry business, now a freedman but once a slave who had helped chisel the marble columns of the temple of Athena Parthenos (Athena the Maiden), the city's patron goddess. The last person in the group was the widow of a wine merchant from the Greek island of Samos; her husband, a resident foreigner, had served in the Athenian army. These four seemed to Pericles to represent all the people who had made Athens the richest, most cultured, and most envied city in Greece.

Now, however, the Greek world was divided into two hostile camps. Attica, Athens's home district in east-central Greece, had been invaded by an alliance of Greek states led by Sparta, the chief city of the Peloponnesus. (The Peloponnesus is a mountainous peninsula that makes up the southernmost area of the Greek continent.) Attica's golden fields of grain were burned; the far-reaching empire that Pericles had struggled so hard to build and hold was threatened. In response, Athens had sent ships south to raid the Peloponnesian coastline near Sparta. No conclusion to the conflict seemed likely for quite some time. Even some of Pericles' friends were beginning to question him: Couldn't he arrange a quick peace with Sparta? Was the war really necessary? For what was Athens fighting?

Pericles stared for a moment at the new graves and then began his address. The heroism of the dead soldiers was obvious, he declared; these men needed no words from him to prove their valor. But, he went on, because it was his duty to give the traditional funeral speech, he would talk about the city, the way of life, and the form of government for which the men had fought.

> *I ask that you fix your eyes on the greatness of Athens. . . . When you realize her greatness, then reflect that what made her great was men with a spirit of adventure, men who knew their duty, men who were ashamed to fall below a certain standard.*
> —PERICLES

15

"Our constitution is called a democracy," he said, "because power is in the hands not of a minority but of the whole people. Everyone is equal before the law." Appointment to public office, he insisted, depended on a person's merit instead of wealth or class connections. Laws were willingly obeyed in the city because they were made by the people instead of by noblemen or tyrants, and because they fairly protected even the poorest of citizens. The Athenians' respect for the law, their civic pride, and their appreciation for things of beauty made the city a magnet for people and products from all over the world.

Pericles then explained the differences between Athens and Sparta. "Our city is open to the world," he said, and noted that Sparta was suspicious of foreigners in its midst. Athens boldly fought its own battles, relying on the innate courage and resourcefulness of its own citizens; Sparta, on the other hand, always gathered its allies together before attacking Athens, and it used a harsh discipline to instill a warlike spirit in its renowned soldiers. Spartans constantly trained for battle, steeling themselves for future troubles, but the Athenians spent their time enjoying cultural activities, working industriously, participating in the city's affairs, and engaging in free thinking debates. Pericles said the Athenian way of life produced a special sense of courage. "The man who can most truly be accounted brave," he said, "is he who knows the meaning of what is sweet in life and what is terrible, and then goes out undeterred to meet what is to come."

Athens's position in the world was clear, said Pericles. "Our city is an education to Greece." No one could claim to be badly governed by this most accomplished of all cities. "Future ages will wonder at us," he predicted, "as the present age wonders at us now." Likewise, the deeds of the dead men lived on in the hearts and memories of the people, earning the fallen heroes the most eternal of all honors. "Famous men," he said, "have the whole earth as their memorial." He reminded his listeners that they were committed to a full-scale war; no matter how great the difficulties that might befall them, they

The goddess Athena was revered as Athens's patron, protector, and namesake. During the Golden Age she was further venerated as goddess of the arts, peace, and prudent wisdom. She was known as the favorite child of Zeus, father of the gods.

could allow no letdown in their resolve. "Happiness depends on being free, and freedom depends on being courageous."

Finally, Pericles spoke to the women in the crowd: "The greatest glory of a woman is to be least talked about by men, whether they are criticizing or praising you." He promised the children of the dead soldiers that Athens would care for them until they had grown up: "This is the crown and the prize that she offers," he said. With a last plea to the people to display their bravest spirits, Pericles departed.

The funeral oration of Pericles is considered to be one of the greatest speeches in all of history. In his address, given in 431 B.C. at the beginning of what was to be a 27-year-long war between Greece's major powers, Pericles tried to inspire his audience by describing some of the special features of Athens that had made it supreme among Greek cities. Like a sculptor using words as a chisel, Pericles carved out an image of a well-rounded Athenian citizen: a man who loved his city, who prized its traditions of democratic government, equitable laws, and freedom of speech, and who exercised both his mind and his muscles while taking part in the city's cultural, commercial, and political affairs. It was not the divine whim of Zeus or one of the other gods that had brought about Athens's rise to greatness, Pericles believed, but the strong character of the people.

Omnipotent Zeus rides in an eagle-drawn chariot with clusters of thunderbolts in his upraised hand. Pericles believed it was hard work and the character of the Athenian people rather than the whim of the gods that had made possible Athens's greatness.

The years of Pericles' leadership of his city are known as the Golden Age of Athens — and of Greece. During this era, in the middle third of the 5th century B.C., a flowering of the arts occurred that is without parallel in the history of Europe. The stunning developments in drama, philosophy, sculpture, and architecture that took place in Periclean Athens formed an intellectual and cultural base on which all of Western civilization rests.

The great artistic triumphs of Greece's golden age were possible because of the peaceful, stable social and political climate in Periclean Athens. Maintaining these conditions in a city that had a strong tradition of free and often heated debate was a masterful feat requiring a person of exceptional ability. Athens was fortunate to have such a man in Pericles, the leader honored by his fellow citizens with the title "the Olympian" — a man worthy of dwelling with the gods on Mount Olympus. Pericles provided a focus for the city's diverse elements, di-

The ideal citizen of Athens prized his city's democratic traditions; he worked industriously, appreciated culture and things of beauty, and engaged in free-ranging debates of political and philosophical issues.

recting the energies of the people toward the glorification of Athens. As he guided Athens through political crises and established programs to foster the arts, his vision of the ideal city and citizen became part of the spirit of Greece's golden age.

More than 24 centuries have passed since Pericles' time, and much of the evidence of the splendor of ancient Athens has been lost, scattered, or reduced to dust. Today historians pore over faded sculptures and shattered vases seeking solutions to questions that have puzzled humanity for ages: Who were the men and women who created the Golden Age of Greece, and why were they able to accomplish so much? Why has their art and thought had such great influence over later civilizations? Why couldn't Pericles prevent the tragic Greek civil war that engulfed his city in the last years of his life? Whatever answers we may find, our inquiries have shown that Pericles was correct — people through the ages have indeed looked back on his city with wonder.

2

The Wooden Walls

On a late-summer day in 480 B.C., the city was in flames. The Great King from the east who had said he would conquer Athens and burn it to ashes had fulfilled his vow. Xerxes, the ruler of the Persian Empire, watched with satisfaction as smoke began to pour from the splendid temples on the peak of the Acropolis, the steep hill in the center of Athens. This troublesome Greek city had dared to stir up rebellion in Persian territories. Now the Great King could exult; his revenge upon Athens would be complete as soon as he had hunted down and enslaved the people who had fled their city. Among these fugitives was Pericles, who was about 13 years old at the time.

At the foot of the Acropolis and in the burning buildings on top of it lay the few men who had chosen to stay and defend Athens against Xerxes' armies. Months before, the oracle of Delphi, the god Apollo's official mouthpiece, had prophesied that Athens would be destroyed and that "the Wooden Walls, they alone will stand." Remembering these words, some stalwarts had barricaded themselves

When we reach Greece I shall destroy the city of Athens. . . . I shall not rest until I have taken Athens and burnt it to ashes.
—XERXES
king of Persia

A Greek youth wearing a victor's crown; from a *stele*, or commemorative pillar, of the 5th century B.C. Greek triumphs over the invading forces of the Persian kings Darius and Xerxes galvanized the resolve of Athenians to preserve their democratic independence.

The Acropolis is the hill overlooking Athens. The burning of Athens by Xerxes in 480 B.C. fulfilled a Delphic prophecy; when prayers to Athena for ultimate victory were answered, the grateful Athenians swore to erect an eternal shrine in her honor upon the sacred hill.

behind wooden doors in the temples of the Acropolis and hurled rocks down upon the attackers. The Persians, however, had broken through the barriers, and Athens's last defenders died leaping from the summit's walls or falling beneath the invaders' spears.

Having destroyed Athens, Xerxes was free to concentrate on his main ambition — the domination of all Greece. Success seemed assured. The opposition was in disarray, divided by petty rivalries and hampered by a lack of organization, and the Greek cities had been unable to mount a strong resistance to the huge Persian army and navy. When Xerxes crossed from Asia into Europe in the spring of 480 B.C., many Greeks had even welcomed the Great King and provided him with troops and supplies. Cities that opposed Xerxes on his march had been burned, their citizens fleeing south across the Isthmus of Corinth to take refuge in the Peloponnesian peninsula. Athens and Sparta had led the fight against the Persians, but Athens was now in ruins and Sparta had lost a king and some of its best warriors in a battle at the mountain pass of Thermopylae in northern Greece.

To the young Athenian Pericles, it must have seemed as though the gods had deserted his people. The son of one of Athens's foremost politicians and generals, he had witnessed his people's frenzied mass exodus overseas to safe havens on the nearby isle of Salamis and in the towns of the Peloponnesus. He had heard of the disagreements among the leaders of the Greek forces and of the Athenian general Themistocles' desperate attempt to keep the alliance from splitting apart. During these dark times, Pericles may well have wondered if he would ever see Athens again.

And yet, though Xerxes had put the torch to Athens, he had not melted the resolve of the Athenians to fight to keep their independence. Within a few weeks of the city's burning, Athens's true wooden walls, the hulls of its ships, would lead the Greek forces in springing a devastating trap on the Persian navy in the Gulf of Salamis, southwest of Athens. His spirit shattered and in fear for his life, Xerxes would flee, leaving behind part of his army to fight his war for him. Emboldened, Greece would then unite to liberate all Greek-speaking people from Persian rule and strip from the Great King the western part of his domain.

> *Leave the high walls that circle your city. . . . Fire and Ares [the god of war] will feed many temples of heaven to the hungry flames. . . . Go from this shrine and teach your souls to weep.*
> —THE ORACLE OF DELPHI delivering a prophecy to Athenian suppliants prior to the Persian invasion

To the Greeks who had fought the invaders, the triumph of their small city-states over the mighty Persian Empire was the most important event in their history. Each city had its heroes from the Persian Wars, and the shared pride in the feats of the cunning generals, brave warriors, and skillful sailors who had turned back the invasion sustained a feeling of unity among the Greeks in the years that followed. The people remembered how their rich cultural tradition and independent spirit had almost been crushed by the all-conquering Persian juggernaut. Such a near loss of their freedom made them prize it even more.

The Greek cities' astonishing victory eventually brought great changes to the lands near the eastern Mediterranean. In Greece and the areas to the east of it, in and around the Aegean Sea, the political order that had connected the various types of states — kingdoms, tyrannies, oligarchies, democracies —

had been shaken up. In the midst of this turmoil a dynamic new force had been unleashed: the power of Athens.

Great cities such as Athens do not arise out of nothing, as Pericles learned in the years following Xerxes' invasion. In Greek myths a king can scatter dragon's teeth on the ground and watch an army spring out of the earth, ready to build him a city. In reality, however, cities grow strong only after many decades or centuries of struggle by generations of people who carry on the hard work of the founders. The Athenians returned from battle in 480 B.C. to a demolished city — the marketplace, gymnasiums, temples, and assembly areas had been razed. But the city's history and traditions were intact in the citizens' minds and hearts, and the Athenians were determined to restore their city to greatness quickly, even without dragon's teeth.

Pericles was far too young to have a noticeable part in the early stages of the rebuilding of his city, but the remarkable energy displayed by the returning Athenians left a deep impression on him. Perhaps even at this early age he was considering ways that this energy could be used to make Athens the shining city that all eyes would turn to, but in these first years after the great invasion Pericles was just one of many Athenian boys struggling at school to memorize the *Iliad* and the *Odyssey*, the great heroic stories by the ancient Greek poet Homer.

The schools Pericles attended in his youth taught boys to read and write, to appreciate fine music and poetry, and to wrestle, run, and throw a javelin. The goal of this educational system was to give the student a strong, upright character. Physical activities were thought to be as important as intellectual pursuits in developing good citizens. A girl's situation, however, was different. Pericles' sister learned the alphabet from her mother, but she did not go to school; she stayed at home, learning to spin, weave, and manage a household.

Whether he was scratching letters on a wax tablet or tossing a javelin, Pericles stood out from other young men because of his distinguished ancestry. He was connected to the Alcmaeonid clan, a family

The Greeks believed that law is an essential element in prosperity because it expresses the will of the gods who watch over it and support it.
—C. M. BOWRA
British historian

that had long played a leading role in the city's politics. His mother, Agariste, was the grandniece of the man who had established democratic rule in Athens. Xanthippus, his father, was prominent in city affairs and had been one of the generals commanding Greek forces at a naval victory during the Persian Wars. Pericles was thus expected to learn all that a man would need to know to gain a high position in Athens's government. One of the most important of these things was a thorough knowledge of the democratic traditions of Athens.

The history of Greece that Pericles learned as a boy was filled with legends about invincible warriors and ferocious monsters; foolish kings and wise lawgivers; and jealous, mischievous gods who sometimes took the form of swans, olive trees, or lightning bolts. These legends emphasized the heroic ideals that all men should strive to follow. Though he might never get the chance, as the immortal Heracles had, to battle nine-headed hydras or wrestle fire-breathing bulls, a young man such as Pericles was taught always to display courage and fortitude

Even among the wealthy and aristocratic classes, women were virtually ignored as democracy in Athens evolved. They received little formal education and, like slaves and foreigners, were not recognized as citizens.

A bust of Homer, the blind epic poet of ancient Greece. His *Iliad* and *Odyssey* were derived from ancient oral narratives. An important part of Pericles' education, they told the tales of the Greek heroes of the Trojan wars and of the gods' interference in human affairs.

so that he could be relied on to defend his city when needed.

Listening to stories of past ages made Pericles aware of the huge debt that the people of his time owed to their ancestors — the men and women who had struggled to win a living from Greece's rocky soil and unpredictable seas. The homeland that the Greeks had fought so hard to save from the Persians was a mountainous peninsula fringed with a jagged coastline stretching out in many regions to long chains of islands.

The rugged and intrepid people who had settled this land had come to Greece in many waves, each group adding to the rich lore of Greek tradition. One legend from very early times told of Theseus, a young man who would become one of Athens's first kings. Taken to Crete — the largest island of Greece, southeast of the mainland — and the splendid palace of Minos, the ruler of the Cretan empire, Theseus had slain the half-human, half-bull monster known as the Minotaur in Minos's mazelike dungeon.

For many centuries the navy of Crete dominated the trade of the seas around Greece. Around 1400 B.C. Crete was rocked by a massive earthquake, and the old sea empire fell to the Mycenaeans, an adventurous people from the Greek mainland. The Mycenaean kings built hilltop fortresses throughout Greece and also sailed eastward across the Aegean Sea to trade or to raid. An expedition led by King Agamemnon against Troy, a city located on the trade route to the Black Sea, later became immortalized in Homer's epic works.

Shortly after 1100 B.C., the Mycenaean civilization crumbled before the Dorians, invaders who swept down from the north and occupied much of Greece. During these invasions many of the peoples living in Greece fled across the Aegean Sea to the areas along the coast of Asia Minor, part of the present-day country of Turkey. The most important area settled by the fugitive peoples was Ionia, a narrow coastal section of western Asia Minor. This region, which would shortly become a center of Greek culture, retained close ties with Attica, the region around Athens that was one of the few areas of the mainland not overrun by the Dorians.

Gradually, throughout the Greek world arose the social unit on which all Greek life would be centered — the city, or *polis*. The mountainous terrain of the Greek mainland isolated the cities from each other; of necessity they became fiercely independent. Because the amount of ground that could be cultivated was limited, satisfying the demand for farmland was a constant problem for the city-states. Many citizens migrated overseas to the Aegean islands and the colonies of Asia Minor. Some groups also moved westward, and by 700 B.C. prosperous Greek cities in Sicily and the Italian peninsula were establishing colonies of their own.

By the 7th century B.C., Greek merchants were regularly sailing to every reach of the Mediterranean to trade their wine, olive oil, linen cloth, and fine pottery and bronze work for grain, lumber, and slaves from other areas. The cities of Ionia and western Asia Minor grew extremely rich, and cultural arts flourished.

In Greece itself, cities vied with each other to gain control of their regions. Inland cities such as Sparta, Thebes, and Argos became land powers, conquering or allying themselves with nearby towns. Other cities, such as Corinth and Aegina, took advantage of their access to the sea to become commercial centers. These bustling, expanding cities were no longer monarchies, that is, ruled by kings; political leadership had passed to councils of oligarchs — the aristocratic landowners and wealthy businessmen who had risen to power in the new conditions. Such governments controlled by the few are known as *oligarchies*.

A very different form of government — democracy — was about to emerge in another city in Greece. Located in the east, five miles from the sea, Athens at first was just one of the many settlements in the district of Attica. Athens slowly gained control over the entire region, however, and the inhabitants of Attica came to look upon themselves as Athenians.

The economy of Athens and Attica was originally based on small farms, but ruling power in the city gradually passed from king to a few aristocratic families, or great houses, who each year elected one man from among them as leader of a governing council.

A wise man anticipates what the future will bring him from observing the experiences of the past.
—SOPHOCLES
Athenian dramatist

Vessel-bearing servants from a fresco at Knossos, the great palace of Minos on the island of Crete. The character of Minoan art is playful and full of rhythmic motion; little is known of the early civilization from which it sprang.

As the great houses gradually built up larger estates, many Athenians lost their land and were driven into poverty and servitude. The protests of the dispossessed farmers finally forced the landowners in 594 B.C. to appoint as *archon*, or chief magistrate, a man of high reputation — Solon the Lawgiver — to carry out reforms.

Solon took a middle course between the demands of the great houses and the small farmers. Recognizing that Athens needed the support of all its citizens to sustain its growth, Solon reorganized the government to give the small farmers a greater voice.

Solon abolished all the debts that had turned poor farmers into servants of the landowners, and he took steps to import grain from overseas to prevent food shortages. On the other hand, although more farmers were admitted to the people's assembly than in the past and thus met to vote on important matters such as declaring war, the chief lawmaking power remained in the hands of the nine archons of the council, a body controlled by the wealthy.

The government of Athens was more representative of the people after Solon's reforms, but fierce contests for political power continued. In the years following the great lawgiver's death, Athens was ruled with absolute authority by the Peisistratid family. Although these and other Greek tyrants, as they are known, were dictators, they were not necessarily bad or harsh rulers and often received strong support from small farmers and tradesmen. The Peisistratids, in fact, governed during a long period of Athenian prosperity. The city's commercial ties with overseas markets grew, and its famed red-figure vases — pottery coated in a black glaze with details painted in red — became a top export item.

By 510 B.C. the tyrants' rule had become increasingly harsh, however, and they had lost all support among the people. The man who commanded the movement to unseat the Peisistratids was the head of one of Athens's leading families, Cleisthenes of the Alcmaeonids. With the help of an army sent by Sparta, the most powerful city in Greece and an enemy of all dictators, Cleisthenes forced Athens's last tyrant to flee abroad.

With Cleisthenes in power the great age of Athenian democracy had truly begun. To prevent political strife among various factions, Cleisthenes divided the citizenry into 10 tribes, each of which contained merchants, farmers, tradesmen, and landowners. The council of 9 was expanded to 500 members, chosen for 1-year terms through a lottery in which all men had an equal chance, rather than by vote. At the same time, the assembly's legislative powers were increased. Ten generals were to be selected each year to carry out the decisions of the

Laws are like spider's webs; if some poor weak creature comes up against them, it is caught; but a bigger one can break through and get away.
—SOLON
Athenian lawgiver

Pottery vats from Knossos. The palace of Minos was both a royal residence and an immense warren of commercial and administrative offices. It survives in Greek legend as the labyrinth of the Minotaur, who was half man and half bull and was slain by Theseus, an early Athenian king.

council and assembly and to lead the city's armies in wartime. To guard against future tyrannies, a provision was made whereby the people could vote to banish, or ostracize, any man who was believed to be a threat to the democratic state.

Cleisthenes' changes naturally were unpopular with certain Athenian aristocratic families who had lost some of their ancient privileges. They called on Sparta, which was afraid of the new democratic government, to send its warriors to Athens to expel Cleisthenes. A Spartan king briefly occupied the city and tried to impose a conservative, oligarchic rule, but the democrats rallied and surrounded the Spartans, forcing them to surrender. Democracy in Athens had passed its first test.

While Athens was evolving into a democratic, commercial city-state (the term refers to both the urban area and its surrounding countryside), developments of great importance were occurring in western Asia Minor. The Greek cities of the region of Ionia had been governed since the 650s B.C. by the fairly benevolent rulers of Lydia, a kingdom in Asia Minor. The Lydians were the first to stamp coins marked with a standard value, and the Ionian cities had borrowed this system and become the richest trading centers of the Greek world. But in 546 B.C. Lydia and Ionia were conquered by the rapidly expanding Persian Empire, whose domain now stretched from central Asia to northern Africa.

The Persians' demands on Ionia for money and troops were heavy, and in 499 B.C. the Greeks of Asia Minor revolted. Only Athens and a few other cities answered the Ionians' appeal to their kinsmen in Greece for help. The Ionians held out for five years before the Persian king, Darius I, crushed the rebellion and incorporated the Ionian ships into his fleet. With western Asia secured, the Great King turned his attention to Athens, the city that had given the most support to the Ionian rebels.

An expedition sent by Darius against Athens crossed the Aegean in 490 B.C., capturing some Greek cities and landing at Marathon in eastern Attica. There, as they reboarded their ships to sail on to Athens, the Persians were surprised by a sudden charge of Athenian *hoplites*, the armored soldiers who formed the backbone of most Greek armies. The Persians died by the thousands on the plain and shores of Marathon, and Darius's fleet was forced to sail back home in defeat.

Although the hoplites had shown themselves to be a match for the most feared warriors in the world, the Athenians knew that the Persians would soon return with an even larger army. Prayers to Athena, guardian of the city, were answered; a huge vein of silver was discovered in the mines at Mount Laurium in Attica, providing Athens with the funds that were so badly needed. Debates raged in the assembly over what to do with the silver. Many wanted to follow the usual practice of sharing public proceeds equally among all citizens, but Themistocles, a politician who had strong support among Athens's lower classes, had another idea. Arguing that the

A red-ware *lekythos*, or oil jar, bears a figure of Nike, the goddess of victory. Greek merchants exported their wine, olive oil, linen, pottery, and bronze to the many lands bordering the Mediterranean Sea.

The Persian empire's king Darius the Great slays a lion. An Ionian revolt against his harsh rule triggered the outbreak of the Persian Wars. Greece's triumph over Persia set the stage for its Golden Age and ensured that it would be Greek values and ideals that served as the foundation of Western civilization.

upcoming conflict would probably be decided at sea, Themistocles convinced the Athenians to use the money to build a fleet of 200 warships and train crews to row them.

Athens's new fleet was ready just in time to face the invasion of Greece by the new Great King, Darius's son Xerxes. Although much of Greece was captured and Athens was punished for its defiance of the Great King, this second expedition ended in disaster for the Persians. The decisive defeat of the Persians in the Gulf of Salamis exposed their vulnerability: with Xerxes humiliated and unable to lead, the Persian army was paralyzed too. The Greeks saw Xerxes' weakness and, like good wrestlers, were quick to press their advantage and start seizing back the Aegean from the Persians.

Solon, Cleisthenes, and the other great leaders of Athens's past had prepared the way for the coming golden age. Their actions and accomplishments served as good lessons to Pericles; problems similar to those faced by his predecessors would trouble him during the half century after Xerxes' invasion — how to strengthen Athens's defenses and supply routes, how to form a government that would satisfy the majority of Athenians, how to maintain a social climate that would encourage the city's arts and industries.

When he became 18, Pericles attended a ceremony marking his passage into Athenian manhood. He had his hair clipped short and from then on would allow his beard to grow. Pericles' education had taught him many lessons about loyalty and leadership, patience and courage. Most of all, though, he had learned to love his city and the proud traditions that had been preserved by the wooden walls of Athens.

3

Silver Owls and Iron Weights

$\mathbf{F}$irst I would like to know, dear friends, where Athens is," says the Persian queen mother Atossa as she awaits the return of her son Xerxes from Greece. The line comes from *The Persians*, a play presented in 472 B.C. by the first great Athenian dramatist, Aeschylus. The play is the oldest complete Greek tragedy that remains today, and it describes the struggle for Greece from the viewpoint of the horrified Persians, who are learning the news of the disaster at Salamis. Like most of the great Athenian plays, *The Persians* was performed at the Dionysia, the festival honoring Dionysus, the god of fertility and wine. Because it is a religious drama, it has a moral theme: the gods' punishment of Xerxes for destroying sacred shrines in Greece and for recklessly trying to extend his empire too far.

The Persians is notable for another reason: the chorus that spoke in order to emphasize the tragedy's plot was paid for by Pericles. Aeschylus was the most famous dramatist in the city, and providing the chorus for his play was a great honor for

> *In common with nearly all Greeks of his time, Pericles considered that a man without a city was a poor and stunted thing. Man makes the city, but the city, and especially Athens, also makes the man.*
> —REX WARNER
> British historian

Pericles committed himself to democratic reforms despite his privileged and conservative background. His handsome appearance was a political asset, as were his family's position, his liberal education, his oratorical abilities, and his patronage of the arts.

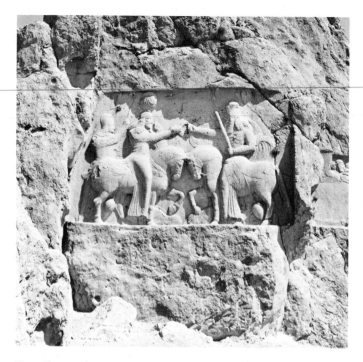

This relief was carved in the cliff wall separating the tombs of Darius and Xerxes. The arrogant belief of the Persian kings in their own invincibility is dramatized in Aeschylus's *The Persians*, which also served as the vehicle for Pericles' entrance into Athenian public life.

Pericles, who was then in his early twenties. Thus art, not politics, gave Pericles his first entry into Athenian civic affairs. He would be a patron of Athens's artists and playwrights throughout his life.

Although by 472 B.C. Pericles had completed his formal education, he still had much to learn about politics and military strategy. Like all Athenian men, after he turned 18 Pericles spent part of the year training with Athens's citizen army. After that, he was ready to grab a spear at any moment and assemble with other men on the wrestling grounds to receive marching orders. Xanthippus, his father, had probably died by this time, so Pericles would have become the head of his family, a young man from a great house with a bright future — if he could avoid the pitfalls of Athens's dangerous political struggles.

For centuries the great houses of Athens had shared power, cooperating with each other to elect the archons who ruled in the council. Once Cleisthenes' democratic reforms were instituted, however, politics became a much wilder affair; the will of the people could no longer be ignored by the lead-

A spectator's seat from an outdoor theater. Athenian plays were premiered in competitions during the annual Dionysia festival, dedicated to the god Dionysus. Dramatists like Aeschylus and Sophocles based their plays on belief in a universal moral order that demanded the intelligent use of power.

ing families. The man who was most successful at gaining popular support was Themistocles. Using his influence with the groups involved in Athens's growing overseas trade, Themistocles was able to have all his chief rivals, including Pericles' father, banished from the city in the decade before Xerxes' invasion. Themistocles' support splintered in postwar Athens, however, and in 471 B.C. his enemies joined forces to drive him from the city forever.

What Pericles thought about the great leader who had guided Athens through the Persian crisis is

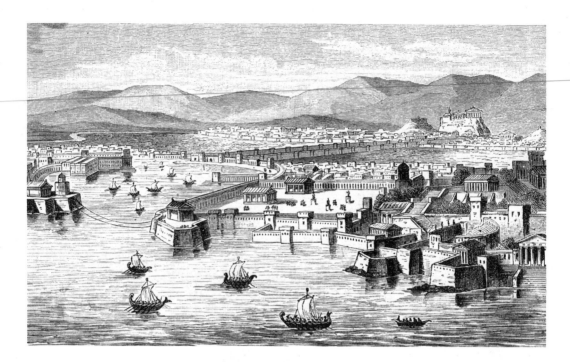

A view of Athens from its
nearby port of Piraeus. The
Long Walls were begun by
Themistocles, hero of Athens's defeat of the Persians
at Salamis in 480 B.C., to defend the cities from attack.
They stretched four miles
from the harbor to the high
hills beyond the Acropolis.

unknown, but he probably admired Themistocles'
intelligent planning and cool nerve. After all, Athens's great strength on the seas had been achieved
because of Themistocles' policies. In addition to
building up Athens's fleet of warships, he had ini-
tiated work on the construction of walls and a dock
area at the nearby city of Piraeus — a port soon to
be the busiest in Greece. Athens's citizens owed a
great deal to him.

Pericles knew that the road to power in Athens
often ended in banishment from the city. He spent
the early years of his manhood as a soldier, safe from
political intrigue, watching Themistocles and other
leaders direct Athens's growing democratic state.
He had time to think about what policies he should
support to win popularity among the voters.

Before standing for election, though, Pericles had
to consider his physical appearance. The voters favored good-looking men, and writers of comic plays
often made vicious fun of a politician with physical
flaws such as a bulbous nose or a potbelly. Pericles
was quite handsome, except for one minor imper-
fection — his head was too big. This distinctive fea-

ture earned him the nickname "Onion head," and busts of Pericles usually depicted him wearing a helmet to hide this flaw.

Despite his overlarge head, Pericles had many good prospects for political success. His city was being transformed; with its strong new walls and booming harbor area, the Athenian metropolis was attracting a steady flow of residents from abroad. Athens's silver coin, the owl-faced *drachma*, was now common currency throughout the Mediterranean. Newly rich sea traders, manufacturers, and mine owners were flocking to the assembly and loudly displaying their knowledge of overseas affairs. Athens's warships were in the midst of carving out a maritime empire, and the landowning aristocrats were losing political power to Piraeus's seamen, merchants, and shopkeepers, the men who earned and traded the "owls."

Pericles was well positioned to take advantage of the new situation — and well trained, too. As a young man privileged to move within the most highly cultured circles of Athenian society, he was able to speak with the many great thinkers from around the Greek world who had come to Athens. His teachers — Damon, Anaxagoras, and Zeno of Elea — forced him to expand his mind and look critically at everything that occurred around him. From these men Pericles learned to keep his passions under control, to analyze problems logically, and to seek natural instead of supernatural causes for such unexplained occurrences as lightning and eclipses.

The influence of Pericles' liberal education won out over his aristocratic ties. In choosing his politics, he sided with democratic reformers who were struggling to expand the rights of the common citizen. As Athens approached an age of expansion and change, with endless opportunities and great dangers, Pericles believed that progressive leaders would be its best guides. His conservative opponents in government feared that a truly democratic system would result in chaos; but Pericles thought otherwise: A proper balance of distinguished leaders and enthusiastic citizenry could make Athens the supreme state in the Greek world.

Here's Pericles, our own onion-headed Zeus
With the Odeum stuck on his head
Like a cap about his ears
—CRATINUS
Athenian comic poet portraying Pericles as the Greek king of the gods wearing a circular, domed theater as a crown

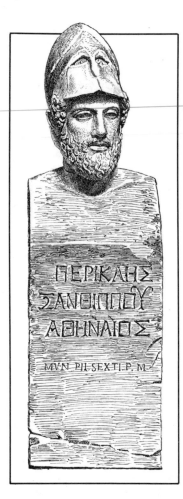

Pericles spent the early days of his career as a soldier, somewhat removed from the turmoil of Athenian politics. Once he entered political life he was a consistent advocate of progressive reform designed to increase the political rights of the middle and lower classes at the expense of the ruling aristocracy.

By the time Pericles entered politics, his city was already well on the way to becoming an imperial power. The war with Persia had continued after the destruction of Xerxes' army, and the Greek cities across the sea in Asia Minor had rebelled and declared their independence. But they still needed the help of a strong navy to protect them from future Persian attacks, and Sparta, long the leading military power in Greece, had only a small fleet and did not want to carry on a long campaign overseas. In addition, Pausanias, a Spartan general who had briefly commanded the united Greek forces in the east, had behaved like a tyrant and made Sparta very unpopular. The Greek cities thus had turned to Athens for leadership in the sacred war against the Persians. Athens had agreed, on the condition that the Greek states in the Aegean form a permanent alliance.

In 477 B.C., representatives from Athens, the Ionian cities in Asia Minor, and most of the Aegean islands met on the isle of Delos to form a confederation of Greek states known as the Delian League. Each of the allies agreed to carry on the war against Persia by providing ships and troops or an annual tribute of money to the league. The league treasury was to be kept at Delos, and the meetings of the delegates were also to be held on the island. The members of the Delian League swore that they would have the same friends and enemies, so Athens, as the confederation's leader, gained a great number of long-term allies. At the end of the first conference, iron weights were dropped in the sea: The league was supposed to last until the weights rose from the Aegean's floor.

The Delian League immediately got to work. Supporters of the Persians were swept from the northern Aegean, and pirates who preyed on Greek merchant ships were driven from their island lairs. As the league expanded its range of operations, more cities on the islands and coasts of the Aegean were invited to join. Some cities willingly became members; others needed to see the prows of the league's warships before joining.

The military leader of the Delian League was the Athenian general Cimon. An aristocrat renowned for his generosity and even temperament, Cimon was also a brilliant war strategist. Taking the finances and military organization of the league firmly in hand, he led the Greeks in a long campaign against the Persian armies in Asia Minor. Finally, in 469 B.C., Cimon's fleet won a crushing land and sea victory over a huge Persian force at the mouth of the Eurymedon River. The Persian threat to the Ionian cities was momentarily ended, and many new cities joined the league, paying tributes that swelled the treasury on Delos.

Cimon's victories, his gifts to the poor, and his free spending to improve Athens's public places made him very popular. His political views were conservative; a supporter of a limited democracy, he believed that the Athenians should let their policies be decided by men like himself, who came from established aristocratic families. In the decade following the exile of Themistocles, Cimon and the other conservatives held power in Athens and resisted any attempts to increase the common citizens' participation in their government. The conservatives made use of the Council of Areopagus, a judicial body composed of former high officeholders, to block new laws supported by Athens's democrats.

Guided by their incorruptible leader Ephialtes and his assistant Pericles, the democrats then mounted a determined attack on the conservatives. They tried Cimon, who had greatly enriched his city with his victories abroad, for having accepted a bribe from the king of Macedon (an ancient country) during a campaign in the north. Pericles was assigned the job of presenting the charge against him at the trial, but he did it halfheartedly, disliking this type of combat. Cimon was acquitted easily. Soon after, however, a natural catastrophe far to the south in the Peloponnesus would help resolve the struggle between Athens's two factions.

The great military state Sparta — an oligarchy ruled in name by its two kings but in reality by its *ephors* (supreme magistrates) and council of elders

Two busts of Pericles have survived. They show the statesman to have been a handsome man, intelligent looking with strong features. Although these portraits may be somewhat idealized, here, we feel, is the Pericles of history—calm, confident, admired, victorious.
—FINLEY HOOPER
American historian

— had dominated the areas around it through its leadership of the Peloponnesian League, a confederation of cities on the peninsula. Though allied with Athens during the Persian Wars, Sparta had become increasingly alarmed over Athens's growing power. The Spartans had advised Athens to stop construction on its defensive walls in the early 470s B.C., but the Athenians had ignored the request, suspecting that Sparta wanted Athens to be unprotected against Peloponnesian invasions of Attica. Although Sparta's armies were nearly invincible, they could not prevent the wind from filling the sails of Athens's fleet. Relations between the two states therefore remained officially friendly but somewhat tense.

In Athens, feelings about the Spartans were mixed. Cimon and the conservatives admired Sparta and were sure that the two leading states could coexist harmoniously. The democrats were suspicious of the Spartans, fearing that they would soon march north and try to impose an oligarchic government like their own on Athens. Pericles was not a confirmed enemy of Sparta — in fact, he was a good friend of Archidamus, the more moderate of its kings — but he knew that the hawkish members of the Spartan council would eventually gain power and try to block further Athenian expansion.

The tensions between the two cities momentarily disappeared in 463 B.C., however, when an earthquake rocked the Peloponnesus and leveled Sparta. Already devastated by heavy losses from the quake, the Spartans were further beset by a rebellion of the *helots*, the local enslaved peasantry, who had banded together to overthrow their masters. Cimon called for his fellow citizens in Athens to send an army to Sparta's aid. The democrats fiercely opposed the mission, hoping that the helots would force their masters to grovel in the dust of the once proud city. But Cimon got his way and led a contingent to help the Spartans regain control of their countryside — something they had already begun to do with a bloody vengeance when the Athenians arrived.

A variety of Greek coins. As Athenian prosperity increased after the defeat of the Persians at Salamis, the Athenian *drachma* — a silver coin with the face of an owl on it — came to embody the Athenian commercial and imperial supremacy throughout the Mediterranean.

In the Peloponnesian city-state of Sparta strict discipline was rigorously imposed on its citizens by an oligarchic government. All Spartan males were trained from childhood to be highly skilled warriors.

With the leader of the conservatives away from Athens, Ephialtes and Pericles decided it was a good time to press their campaign for democratic reforms. A measure was successfully carried through the assembly to strip the conservative Council of Areopagus of most of its functions. This victory clearly demonstrated the strength of the democrats' support and opened the way for further legislation.

Meanwhile, with the help of troops from friendly states, the Spartans finally stamped out all but a few pockets of rebellion in the southern Peloponnesus. The dreary stone barracks that constituted so much of the garrisonlike city of Sparta were soon being reconstructed. Secure once again, the Spartans decided that the relief force from democratic Athens was a bad influence on their allies, and Cimon was rudely ordered to take his men home.

The Athenians greeted Cimon angrily on his return, blaming him for letting their city be insulted by Sparta. When he attempted to halt the passage of further democratic programs in the assembly, a majority of the people decided he must go. In 461 B.C. Cimon was banished from his city for 10 years. The democrats were jubilant, but their joy was soon checked. In retaliation for Cimon's exile, the conservatives had Ephialtes assassinated.

With Ephialtes and Cimon removed from the scene, Pericles was in a strong position to play a leading role in Athenian politics. The elders in the democrats' upper ranks were beginning to step aside for the rising young politician, clearly recognizing that he was the man best able to lead Athens in the years ahead. In the meantime, the Athenians were venturing out in many directions. Future conflicts between Athens and other Greek states seemed inevitable, and spears were being sharpened. But while peace reigned, goods flowed into the port at Piraeus from around the Mediterranean. Twenty years before, the Persian queen mother had learned where Athens was; soon the name of Pericles' city would be known everywhere.

Cimon, the conservative military leader of the Delian League. His popularity in Athens was undermined and eventually destroyed by his resistance to democratic reforms; he was exiled from the city after eight controversial years in power.

4

A Dangerous Empire

During the 20 years following the Persian invasion, relations between the two great city-states in Greece had remained relatively peaceful. That fragile unity had been shaken apart by 460 B.C., however, and a 15-year period of wars and uneasy truces between the "allied" confederations of Athens and Sparta was beginning. The humiliating return of Cimon's relief force from the Peloponnesus had ended any chance for cooperation between the powers. The Spartan-Athenian competition grew more intense, and other Greek states were pulled into a conflict that was fed by old fears and hostilities and new grievances and suspicions.

The conservatives had been swept from power in Athens and the democrats were in control. Pericles was their leading spokesman, but he shared the leadership of Athens in this new time of struggle with other men, many of them veterans of the Persian Wars. These men remembered the victories they had gained against seemingly impossible odds, and they favored an aggressive foreign policy on almost all fronts. Pericles' task was to help construct

Great as Athens had been when he became her leader, he made her the greatest of all cities, and he came to hold more power in his hands than many a king or tyrant.
—PLUTARCH
Greek historian

Exquisitely carved *Caryatids*, or female figures, support a roof of the Erechtheum sanctuary near the Parthenon. Architecture and sculpture flourished in Athens during the Age of Pericles.

Athenian and Corinthian *hoplites* — soldiers in armor — depicted in combat on a Greek vase. The growth of Athenian power brought hostility and suspicion from the rival Greek states. War between Corinth and Athens broke out when Athens attempted to establish bases in the Peloponnesus.

a program that would satisfy the men of his own party without alienating the conservatives.

Now well established in Athenian political circles, Pericles was also a husband, father, and the owner of a large estate. He had married a near relative and by her had two sons, Xanthippus and Paralus. His relationship with his wife and children was never very close; his sons thought their father was overbearing, and his marriage would end in divorce some years later. Perhaps because he was so absorbed in civic affairs, Pericles had little time for his family. He did not pay much attention to his landholdings either, leaving the management of the farm work to a servant.

Although he was unsuccessful at dealing with the people in his own home, Pericles was without equal as a public speaker and political negotiator. He forcefully pressed his views on the assembly, supporting measures that would protect Athens from attacks by Sparta and other hostile states. He advocated blocking off invasion routes to Attica and securing Athens's overseas grain supplies, two actions that were imperative if the city was to increase its power. To accomplish these ends Athens would have to seize control of areas claimed by other cities, and by 460 B.C. Pericles and the Athenians were prepared for a major war.

The field of contest in the battle for Greek supremacy was to be centered on the Isthmus of Corinth, the narrow strip of land connecting the Peloponnesus with the Greek mainland. The important naval battles would be fought in the two bodies of water surrounding the isthmus. To the west was the long, narrow Gulf of Corinth; to the east lay the Saronic Gulf, the home waters of Athens and the island of Aegina. Hostilities began when Athens formed an alliance with Megara, an isthmus city formerly allied with Sparta. Megara was at war with the powerful neighboring city of Corinth, and Athens's interference in the dispute earned it the deep hatred of a people with a long memory. The Corinthians would begin to exact their revenge three decades later. For the moment, however, the Athenians gained huge advantages. They built a wall from the Saronic Gulf to the Gulf of Corinth, thereby blocking the isthmus against invading armies. Athens also received access to a port on the Gulf of Corinth and quickly began setting up naval stations farther to the west.

A full-scale war broke out when Athens attempted to establish bases in the Peloponnesus. Alarmed by the Athenian expansion, Corinth and Aegina united in a campaign to drive Athens out of their waters. After a few small encounters, the fleet of Athens and its allies met with Aegina's fleet and crushed it. The island city was soon under siege.

With its ally in deep trouble, Corinth tried to relieve the pressure on Aegina. Knowing that most of

The secret of Pericles' power depended not merely upon his oratory, but upon the reputation which his whole course of life had earned him.
—PLUTARCH
Greek historian

49

the Athenian troops were far from home, the Corinthians drove toward Megara and the new wall that barred the way to Attica. Extreme measures were necessary in Athens. A general named Myronides gathered retired army veterans and boys too young for regular service and marched to meet the invaders. Age and youth combined to rout the Corinthians, and the Athenians' pride in their army swelled enormously.

Under its new democratic leadership, Athens was being kept busy on many fronts. Pericles and his fellows now began a building project that would make the city nearly invulnerable to siege. Construction started on the Long Walls, stone fortifications running southward for nearly four miles and connecting Athens to its port at Piraeus. Soon, no enemy would be able to block Athens's access to supplies from overseas — as long as the city's navy remained strong.

Although involved in a fierce battle with neighboring states, Athens managed to take part in a war on the other side of the Mediterranean. In Egypt, the ancient kingdom that had been conquered by Persia in 525 B.C., a revolt had broken out in 461 B.C. against Xerxes' successor, Artaxerxes. Ever ready to harass the Persians and move into a rich commercial region, Athens and its allies in the Delian League had sent a large military force to help the Egyptian rebels. An Athenian-Egyptian fleet had sailed up the Nile and taken much of northern Egypt from the Persians, but the conflict turned into a stalemate. Athens was bogged down in a distant overseas campaign just as the situation at home became very dangerous.

Still recovering from its losses during the earthquake, Sparta had been slow to challenge Athens. In 458 B.C., however, one of Sparta's allies in northern Greece was threatened by a neighboring state. Using the opportunity to go on the march, the Spartans ferried a large force across the Gulf of Corinth before an Athenian fleet could intervene. The Spartan army quickly squashed its ally's opponent and then turned to its main objective: a confrontation with the Athenians.

With your navy as it is today there is no power on earth—not the king of Persia nor any people under the sun—that can stop you from sailing where you wish.

—PERICLES
speaking to the Athenians

The Spartans marched south and entered Boeotia, the district to the northwest of Attica. The ruling oligarchs in Thebes, the largest Boeotian city, offered to support Sparta if it would help the Thebans gain control over its neighbors. The Spartans agreed to the plan, hoping to establish a strong anti-democratic, anti-Athenian confederation on Attica's borders.

The atmosphere in Athens was very tense. The Long Walls were only partially completed, and some of the conservative aristocrats in Athens were reported to favor Sparta's attempt to overthrow their city's democratic government. For Pericles and the loyal majority of Athenian citizens, a head-on en-

An Egyptian funerary sculpture. With the aim of gaining access to Egypt's enormous agricultural wealth, Athens diverted military forces from its struggle with Corinth to aid an Egyptian rebellion against Persia.

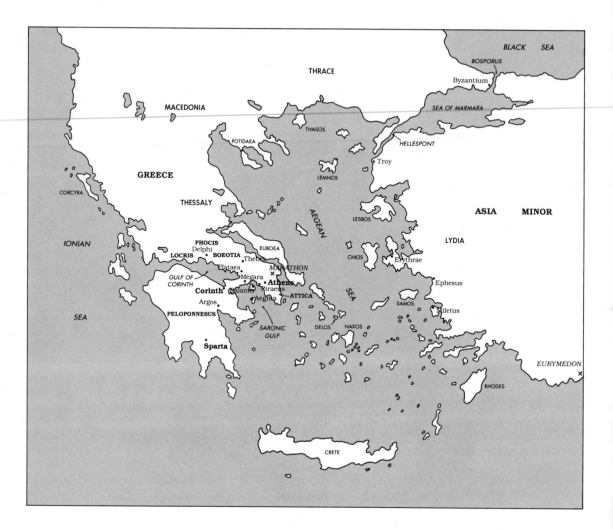

By the 470s B.C. Athenian naval power had established a far-flung empire around the Aegean sea, enabling Athens to prosper through trade and commerce.

counter with the menace at Attica's doorstep was the only possible course of action.

The Athenian army that assembled to march into Boeotia was slightly larger than the Spartan force, but every man in it knew he would be facing the best warriors in Greece. The mighty city-states were destined to meet in battle many more times before the century ended. Sparta was fighting to maintain the old conservative political order, in which the word of the few was law. The Athenians were seeking to preserve their democratic constitution and to create a new order that would revolve around Athens's sea empire.   The opposing armies formed two lines just outside of Attica, near the Boeotian city of Tanagra. The Athenians were supported by allied contingents of cavalrymen from Thessaly, a region in the north, and foot soldiers from the Peloponnesian city of Argos, one of Sparta's oldest enemies. Shortly before the battle began, the exiled general Cimon appeared in armor in front of the Athenians, asking to be allowed to fight for his city. Afraid that Cimon might regain his popularity, Pericles made sure that the request was denied, accusing the banished aristocrat of being pro-Spartan. Cimon gracefully accepted the rejection of his plea, telling a group of his friends to fight extra hard for his sake. His display greatly heartened the Athenians.

The Battle of Tanagra was a bloody affair, with both sides suffering heavy losses. Cimon's band of friends died to the last man, and Pericles, not to be outdone, fought with special ferocity. The Spartans gained the upper hand on the battlefield when the Thessalians switched to their side. Even so, the Spartans could not follow up their costly triumph. They limped homeward, forcing a passage through the Isthmus of Corinth.

The battle helped to unify Athens; conservatives and democrats, commoners and aristocrats could all rejoice in having fought Greece's most feared warriors to a virtual draw. No acts of treason had been attempted, and many Athenians were sorry that they had banished the loyal Cimon. Hoping to heal old factional wounds, Pericles proposed that Cimon be recalled from exile, a move that was popular with the people. The two men reached an accord, and Cimon was sent on a mission to the Peloponnesus, where he used his good relationship with the Spartans to negotiate a truce.

Sparta was hoping that the recall of Cimon meant that Athens was now interested in a lasting peace, but its hopes were soon shattered. In Athens, confidence in the city's military might was boundless, and the leaders of prowar factions convinced the Athenians to use the four-month truce period engineered by Cimon and Pericles to invade Boeo-

Pericles believed that Athens was destined to become the dominant Greek state. After the Battle of Tanagra he moved to unite Athens's political rivals by recalling Cimon from exile. Cimon served as an emissary to Sparta while Athens used its naval power to expand its empire.

Figures on the east frieze of the Parthenon. The uncertain loyalties of conservative aristocrats caused the political atmosphere in Athens to grow tense as Sparta moved to overthrow the city's democratic government, but Sparta withdrew after the Battle of Tanagra in 457 B.C.

tia. Thrusting northward against the hostile states beyond the Attic border, Athenian forces under Myronides routed a Boeotian army led by Thebes at the Battle of Oenophyta. Athens gained control of Boeotia and its neighboring districts of Phocis and Locris, and quickly established friendly democratic governments in cities throughout the occupied territories. Athens was now clearly the dominant power in Greece.

The surrender of the island of Aegina to the besieging Athenian forces in the spring of 457 B.C. completed a series of stunning triumphs for Athens. Aegina was forced to become a tribute-paying member of the Delian League. Athens kept up the pressure on Sparta and Corinth during the rest of that year and the two years following, raiding ports in the Peloponnesus and seizing more towns on the Gulf of Corinth. The Long Walls were completed, further strengthening Athens's defenses.

Twenty-five years after Salamis, the Athenians were starting to believe that they were destined to rule Greece. Athens's control over the Delian League had become ever more forceful, turning what had once been a union of free states into little more than an imperial confederation. Expanding its borders, Athens had conquered many potential trouble spots. It would face a severe crisis if its new subject states should ever rise in a concerted revolt, but for the moment the Athenians were supremely confident. Their optimism was best reflected in the man they were about to install as first citizen: Little by little, the people of Athens were beginning to share Pericles' vision of the city and its empire.

Pericles, because of his position, his intelligence, and his known integrity, could respect the liberty of the people and at the same time hold them in check. It was he who led them, rather than they who led him.
—THUCYDIDES
Athenian historian

5

Necessary Expenditures

From a ruin deserted by its own people after Xerxes' revenge a quarter century before, Athens had become an imperial power that could attract the services of men from all over the world. At the same time, the city had gained the envy and hatred of its neighbors, and Sparta, Corinth, and Thebes were waiting impatiently for a chance to humble Athens. Though fully aware of the hostility they had aroused, the Athenians were sure that all the Greek states would eventually come to appreciate the political stability and cultural benefits enjoyed by Athens's allies. Even more, Pericles hoped to form a confederation that would unite all the Greeks.

By 454 B.C. Pericles had been a leading figure in Athenian politics for more than six years and, like his empire, had gained numerous enemies and allies. In that year he was elected general, and thus he was one of the 10 men directly responsible for carrying out the decisions of the council and assembly. (Although Pericles may have been a general before, this is the first year that Plutarch, the Greek

All who have taken it upon themselves to rule over others have incurred hatred and unpopularity for a time; but if one has a great aim to pursue, this burden of envy must be accepted.
—PERICLES
on Athens's relationship
with its allies

Athena was worshiped throughout Greece, but her special cults flourished in Athens. Three temples devoted to her were built on the Acropolis under Pericles' massive public building plan: the Parthenon, the Erechtheum, and that of Athena Nike.

A delicately painted black-figure urn depicts mythic heroes playing dice. As a result of sea commerce, Athenian pottery became a highly valued trading commodity throughout the Mediterranean, the Middle East, and North Africa.

historian who is our main source of biographical information on Pericles, records that he held that position.) From that point on, the hand that guided Athens's state policies was Pericles', and it was to him that the Athenians would turn in times of crisis. As the most powerful figure on the board of generals, he would at times exercise seemingly complete control over Athenian politics.

In a state run by citizens of widely varying backgrounds — men who often differed greatly in their political views and who delighted in taking advantage of their right to do so — some degree of internal strife was inevitable. Reaching agreement on state policy was sometimes difficult; a decision made by the assembly on one day might be reversed on the next when a particularly effective speaker, such as Pericles, presented the case in a new light. The main danger to Athenian democracy was that one group might gain enough popular support to dominate the assembly and suppress all viewpoints that differed from its own.

Although the Athenians' intense love for their city held it together in spite of the divergent forces flowing within it, the conflict between the conservatives and the democrats was fueled by broad divisions in Athenian society. The conservatives, whose main support lay among the aristocratic landowners and farmers of Attica, were uneasy about the great changes occurring in Athens. Their main concerns were agricultural, and they distrusted expansionist wars that might bring an avenging enemy army into Attica to burn their olive groves and wheat fields. They also believed that a freedom-loving state such as Athens should not impose its will on other cities. The democrats, supported by the city's merchants and tradesmen, concentrated on securing more overseas markets for Athenian wares. They fought to expand the political rights of the common citizen and made sure that large numbers of Athenians — men who would vote for them — were employed in the fleets. The democrats tended to favor an aggressive policy against Athens's rivals, and they took a hard line on punishing disloyal allies in the Delian League.

In addition to the voting population, other groups greatly affected Athenian society. Citizens of many Greek cities had flooded into Athens to settle. Known as *metics*, they were active in trading and manufacturing. They were not allowed to participate in the government, but the metics could fight in the military and had some influence in politics. Also vital to Athens were the slaves who labored in mines and workshops and tended the fields of the great estates. Without the services of their slaves, many Athenian citizens would not have had so much free time to spend on civic affairs. Some slaves eventually won their liberty, and these freedmen became an important part of the work force. Lastly, there were the women. With little or no opportunities open for them in business or government, most women raised families and ran households.

Themistocles had tried to control Athens by having his opponents banished; but Pericles tried a different approach: He sought to unite the city's different elements behind a program designed to

During the whole period of peacetime when Pericles was at the head of affairs, the state was wisely led and firmly guarded, and it was under him that Athens was at her greatest.
—THUCYDIDES
Athenian historian

A 19th-century drawing depicts prisoners of war being auctioned in the ancient Athenian slave market. Slaves played an important part in the culture of Athens by affording their owners the free time to participate in public affairs.

promote Athenian strength and security. The Athenian treasury had grown enormously, and Pericles dipped into the public funds, winning wide support by having laws passed that allowed citizens to be paid while sitting on juries and getting measures approved that allowed for salaries for soldiers, sailors, and certain government officials. The democrats also enacted further measures that were popular with the Athenian masses, such as opening the honored but largely ceremonial position of archon to all citizens.

Although the aristocrat Pericles had firmly entrenched himself as the leader of the common citizens, he maintained strong ties with his own class and worked to dilute the opposition of the great families to democratic reforms. With Athens still at war, Pericles needed the backing of his fellow generals and the members of the council, many of whom were aristocrats. Cimon was not on the scene. Opposed to Athens's war with other Greek states, the conservative leader had chosen to finish out his term of exile abroad.

Still hoping to gain control of the Gulf of Corinth, Pericles mounted his first campaign as general in

454 B.C. Raiding along the northern and southern shores of the gulf, Pericles punished a number of cities that had been hostile to Athens. Grim news from Egypt, however, brought an end to any further Athenian campaigns in Greece. A Persian army had crushed the Egyptian revolt, and almost the entire Athenian force there had been destroyed.

The Egyptian disaster cost Athens the peace it had maintained in the Aegean. Two cities in Ionia, Erythrae and the important trading center of Miletus, tried to break away from the Delian League. In both places the revolts were started by Persian sympathizers who hoped to take advantage of Athens's setback in Egypt and establish themselves as tyrants in their home cities. Like all previous rebellions within the league, these uprisings were soon put down, and Pericles and his fellow generals moved quickly so that the unrest did not spread. The Athenian fleet ousted both dictators, and friendly governments were installed — a democratic state in Erythrae and an oligarchic regime in Miletus.

As the arrangement with the Milesian aristocrats shows, Pericles was more interested in working to insure stable relations with governments in allied cities than he was with forcing democracies on unwilling states. Persian meddling in affairs of the Delian League alarmed the Athenians, however; stability was threatened and the treasury on the tiny island of Delos was vulnerable to seizure. Athens convinced its allies that a change was necessary. Over the years an increasing number of league members had found it easier to pay their annual fees in gold rather than in troops and ships; now the treasury's *talents* (currency unit equal to a huge amount of gold) were moved to the fortified Athenian Acropolis, and part of the annual tribute collected from league members was henceforth to be paid to Athena, the organization's new official patron goddess.

With the league's funds safe, Athens was in an even better position to dominate its allies than before. Athens's navy had assumed an ever-larger role in league affairs, often forcing reluctant allies to pay

Pericles constantly strove to curb the Athenians' extravagant spirit of conquest . . . and to devote Athens's main strength to guarding and consolidating what she had already won.
—PLUTARCH
Greek historian

Pericles mounted his first campaign as general — he was elected to the post in 454 B.C. — in an attempt to gain control of the Gulf of Corinth. By 446 B.C. Pericles had established peace with Persia and Sparta, Athens's most dangerous rivals.

overdue bills. Despite their grumbling about the tribute, however, most league members believed that the advantages of Athens's protection outweighed the costs. In addition, the league cities were made to feel as if they were active participants in an Athenian confederation. Each was invited to take part in the Great Panatheniac Festival honoring Athena, which occurred every four years.

Once the Aegean was again secure and league revenues were restored to normal, Pericles decided it was time to end hostilities with Sparta. Athens was clearly overextended and needed to lose a few of its enemies. Cimon had returned from his exile, and Pericles asked him to lead another peace mission to Sparta. Reassured by Cimon's presence, the Spartans agreed in 451 B.C. to honor a five-year truce with Athens. Cimon probably told the Spartans that Athens would renew the war with Persia; indeed, he was soon dispatched with a large fleet to attack Persian forces on the island of Cyprus. After winning a few battles with the Persian navy, Cimon fell ill and died. Although forced to break off the campaign in Cyprus, the Athenians inflicted another defeat on the Persians, a victory dedicated to the memory of their great commander.

Cimon was the unsurpassed military leader of the time; Pericles, the supreme statesman. Often adversaries, the two men nonetheless had managed to work together on occasion. Both placed their loyalty to Athens above personal or political disagreements. Cimon's death was a huge blow to Athens, and it left the conservatives leaderless. Pericles further divided the opposition by having measures passed that pleased the moderate conservatives, such as one limiting citizenship to those whose parents were Athenian. This law reduced the number of people eligible for state benefits, and though popular with Athenian citizens, in the long run it probably weakened the empire. Pericles would later have personal reasons for regretting the passage of the citizenship law.

His position free from serious challenge, Pericles now tried two diplomatic ventures that he hoped would safeguard the Athenian Empire. Believing that further actions against Persia would be unwise, Pericles sent Callias, brother-in-law of Cimon, to the Persian capital at Susa to negotiate a peace settlement with King Artaxerxes. A treaty was signed in 449 B.C., ending more than 40 years of warfare between the two states.

Having achieved peace in the east, Pericles attempted to bring about the Greek unity he had long dreamed of. Ambassadors were sent to all the major Greek states, asking them to send representatives to a panhellenic (all-Greek) congress in Athens. Sparta, unwilling to accept Athens's leading role in the panhellenic movement, frustrated Pericles' efforts, and the congress never met. His attempt to unify Greece had failed, but Pericles had gained a diplomatic victory. Sparta had been made to look bad—as if it didn't care about the welfare of Greece.

Pericles planned a cultural triumph as well. One of the matters that was to have been discussed at the congress was the construction of Greek temples destroyed by Xerxes. No other city was offering to help Athens restore its temples, so Pericles decided to begin a rebuilding program using available funds. "Available funds" meant the Delian League treasury.

Gold talents were accumulating in the league's storage vaults in Athens. The annual tribute was still collected by Athens even though the purpose for which it was earmarked — the war with Persia — no longer existed. If league unity and the tribute were allowed to slip, Pericles and the democrats insisted, so too would the alliance's defenses, and the Persians would move back into the Aegean. In the meantime, employment had to be found for some of the soldiers and sailors thrown out of work by the recent peace treaties. Pericles intended to make the Acropolis a splendid showcase of Greek art and religious devotion, and he believed that most of Athens's allies would be glad to contribute to the city's public works project. Backed by popular support, construction began.

Just as peace seemed complete throughout Athens's empire, trouble flared. Despite the truce between Athens and Sparta, the Spartans were not content to let Athens have the upper hand in Greek affairs. Now that Athens had signed a peace treaty with Artaxerxes, Sparta could attack its rival without being accused of helping the Persians. In 449 B.C. the Spartans seized from one of Athens's allies the sacred oracle of Delphi, the shrine at the foot of

> *If you will not listen to me then listen to Time, which is the most experienced of all counselors.*
>
> —PERICLES
> advising his fellow general
> Tolmides to postpone his
> attempt to
> recapture Boeotia

A view of the ruins of Delphi, site of the most influential oracle. Ambassadors were sent to consult the Delphic oracle with questions of political import; the answers, often difficult to interpret, were believed to be the words of Apollo, god of prophecy.

Mt. Parnassus, where answers to human questions asked of the god Apollo were spoken by a priestess. Sparta then installed its own allies as protectors of Apollo's temple. Thereafter, Sparta was able to sway the oracle's prophecies against Athens. Hoping that tensions would subside, Pericles waited two years before restoring Athenian control over Delphi.

The real crisis for Athens began in Boeotia. Anti-Athenian sentiment had been growing in many cities in that district, and in 446 B.C. a group of oligarchs in the city of Thebes organized a full-scale revolt. Pericles saw that there was no hope of immediately regaining Boeotia, but he was unable to prevent the veteran general Tolmides from gathering a small army of eager young men and marching northward. A rebel army ambushed the overconfident Athenians near the Boeotian town of Coronea, killing Tolmides and capturing a large number of prisoners, many of them the sons of Athens's most prominent families. To win the captives' release,

A detail from "The Charioteer of Delphi" shows the face of a young competitor in a ritual chariot race conducted for the divine favor of Apollo. Both Sparta and Athens believed themselves blessed by the gods and destined to dominate Greece. The Thirty Years' Peace signed in 446 B.C. temporarily ended their hostility.

Athens agreed to recall its troops from all the districts north of Attica, which it had occupied 12 years before.

Unrest continued to grow, however, and the Athenians were soon fighting desperately for their lives and their empire. Cities on the Aegean island of Euboea revolted. Pericles could not let this important territory directly to the east of Attica slip from Athens's control, and he quickly led an expedition to stamp out the rebellion. No sooner had he begun his campaign through Euboea, however, when terrifying news reached him. The isthmus city of Megara had allied itself with Corinth and Sparta and massacred the Athenian garrison stationed there. The five years' truce between Athens and Sparta had just expired, and the Spartans immediately sent an army under Pleistoanax, their young king, to ravage Attica. Pericles was forced to hurry home to face the menace on Athens's doorstep.

Wishing to avoid a costly battle that might leave Athens too weak to hold onto its empire, Pericles tried to negotiate with the Spartans. Surprisingly, little effort was needed to persuade Pleistoanax to leave Attica. The relieved Athenians had hardly begun thanking Pericles for saving the city before he was back in Euboea. The revolt was suppressed, and to avoid future trouble on the island Pericles established settlements of loyal Athenian citizens on land taken from Euboean rebels.

In the course of a few months during 446 B.C., Athens's dreams of building an empire on the Greek mainland had disappeared. Clearly, Sparta had organized the concerted uprisings, hoping that the Athenian alliance would be pulled apart. Athens retained its hold over the Aegean, but Sparta had now reasserted itself as the dominant influence on the mainland. The two states were now eager to solidify their positions, and in the winter of 446–445 B.C. the Thirty Years' Peace was signed. Both cities agreed not to interfere with the other's allies. Disputes were to be settled through arbitration.

Pericles needed all his diplomatic skills to persuade the more militaristic Athenians to give up the struggle to control Greece. Winning concessions from the stubborn and cautious Spartans had also been tough. But Pericles had prevailed, and he was now able to concentrate on his rebuilding program and on Athens's relations with its allies.

Most of the Greeks were relieved that they could go about their business without keeping an eye open for raiding warships and invading armies. There were some in the Spartan council, however, who were sure that Pericles had bribed Pleistoanax to take his army home, allowing Athens to escape with its empire mainly intact. Thus, when the king returned to Sparta, the council fined him so heavily that he went into exile. Probably it was Pericles' assurance that Athens was willing to agree to peace at terms favorable to Sparta, rather than a gift of gold, that had persuaded Pleistoanax to leave, but at the end of the year, when Pericles presented an account of his campaign expenses to the assembly, it included one mysterious entry: "For necessary expenditures: 10 talents."

6

An Education to Greece

Peace reigned throughout Greece, but the Athenians were, as a Corinthian ambassador to Sparta complained, "by nature incapable of leading a quiet life." Athens was not to be a tranquil city. The new battleground was the *agora* — the central marketplace — where the greatest minds in Athens gathered to argue, listen, and teach. Daily, amid the hubbub arising from the agora's shops and stalls, the men of Athens met to discuss such matters as new alliances with foreign states, the designs of temples being built on the Acropolis, and the merit of the dramas being presented at the Dionysia Festival. Further discussions took place at the jury courts; at the Theater of Dionysus; in the Pnyx, where the assembly met; and in the gymnasia, the shady groves around the city where young men were educated. Out of them came the intellectual fervor that gave birth to the Golden Age of Athens.

This great era of artistic achievement is also known as the Age of Pericles. Although he never sculpted a masterpiece such as Myron's bronze

When Archidamus, the king of Sparta, asked Thucydides whether he or Pericles was the better wrestler, Thucydides replied: "Whenever I throw him at wrestling, he beats me by arguing that he was never down, and he can even make the spectators believe it."
—PLUTARCH
Greek historian recording the conservative leader Thucydides' analogy about his debates with Pericles

A detail from the Parthenon exemplifies the meticulous refinements of Greek sculpture. During the Age of Pericles the Athenian workshops that rebuilt the Acropolis created a lasting tribute to their city's artistry.

Athena and Marsyas, never wrote a play that could move an audience like Sophocles' *Oedipus at Colonos*, and never designed a building to stand as proudly a Mnesicles' Propylaea, Pericles can nevertheless claim a major share of the credit for his city's cultural flowering. A man of both thought and action, Pericles relied on Athens's artists and thinkers for advice and inspiration. He, in turn, provided a nurturing environment for their work, and it is he who must be thanked for the monuments that sat on the Acropolis, Athens's high holy place, proclaiming the glory of classical Athens long after most of the other famous works of the period were lost.

Constantly reminded by Pericles that they were special, favored by the gods, and supreme in art and war, the Athenians devoted themselves to their city.

The *agora* of Athens was the centerpiece of the city's public life. Surrounded by markets, shrines, and government buildings, it was an open-air forum where citizens of Athens's free society met to discuss current issues.

Every citizen felt blessed to be living in the state with the fairest laws and best government and believed that no sacrifice was too heavy if performed in the noble cause of adding to Athens's glory. Pericles' words instilled in them the confidence that they could achieve new levels of greatness.

The construction on the Acropolis began in the early 440s B.C. Almost every Athenian was drawn to some degree into Pericles' grand project, and many men were employed full-time in the jobs of erecting and decorating Athens's new temples. Stone cutters, wagon drivers, rope makers, sailors, and road builders joined hundreds of other workers in preparing and transporting marble, gold, bronze, ivory, and cypress wood to the Acropolis. Architects, masons, painters, weavers, coppersmiths, carpenters,

The tragedies of the great playwright Sophocles moved his audiences to a *catharsis*, or cleansing of the emotions; his use of mythic figures ennobled universal human dilemmas. Athens during its Golden Age fostered outstanding achievements in all art forms.

A gold funeral mask of a Mycenaean king from the 16th century B.C. The stiff, formalized styles of earlier Greek art was replaced during the Golden Age by natural vitality that celebrated the human form.

and sculptors formed the raw materials into finished masterworks. The craftsmen constantly refined their techniques, creating works of such beauty that artists of later centuries would consider them the standard of perfection and copy them endlessly.

The building program was the greatest undertaking of Pericles' career, and he kept a close watch over the construction at all stages. He wanted no one to complain that stacks of gold talents had bought only second-rate work or that the goddess Athena would judge the products to be unworthy of her. Visits to craftsmen's studios helped him assess who had the best techniques. He chose men of great vision — architects such as Pheidias, Ictinus, and Callicrates — to design the new temples. His boundless energy inspired the workers and made the Athenians feel that they were involved more in a sacred mission than an immense public works program.

Once begun, the buildings arose with amazing speed, though some would not even be started during Pericles' lifetime. The master plan called for a wide stairway to lead up from the gates in the Acropolis's western walls into the monumental building that served as an entrance way to the summit, the high-columned Propylaea. Straight beyond was Pheidias's huge bronze statue, *Athena Promachos*

(Athena, First in Battle), holding a spear whose gleaming tip could be seen by sailors far out at sea. At the top of the peak was the famed Parthenon, Athena's main temple and an architectural masterpiece. Scattered below were more shrines honoring the goddess of wisdom and her fellow deities Zeus, the supreme god; Poseidon, god of the sea; and Artemis, the huntress and goddess of the wild. Most famous of these other temples was the Erechtheum. Built of marble on the spot where Poseidon and Athena supposedly staged a contest to decide which of them would be the city's protector, the Erechtheum's porches were supported by columns in the shape of maidens known as Caryatids.

Whether viewed from far or near, the Acropolis's point of focus was the Parthenon. Built between 447 and 438 B.C., this majestic temple was fashioned by the hands of Athens's most skilled craftsmen using the best marble available. Because straight lines appear to curve when observed from a distance, the

The majestic Parthenon is the focal point of the Acropolis. The interior was dominated by a towering statue of Athena, made entirely of gold and ivory by the sculptor Pheidias; friezes at each exterior end depict scenes from myth and history.

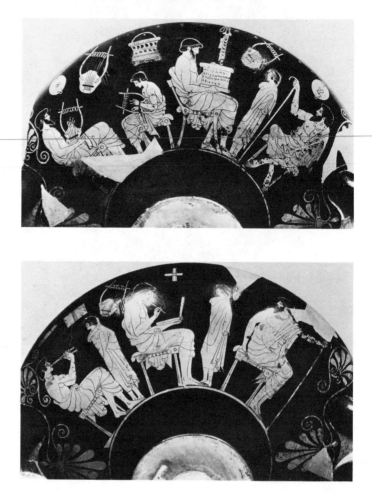

A bowl decorated with scenes of students being instructed by their tutors in music and literature. The prosperity and enlightened environment of Athens during ther Golden Age enabled some citizens, like the great philosophers Plato and Socrates, to devote their entire lives to the pursuit of knowledge.

architects designed the Parthenon's columns to have a slight compensatory bulge in the middle. Sculptured surfaces decorating the triangular space below the points of the roof at each end of the temple depicted traditional subjects: the birth of Athena; battles between gods and giants, Amazons and Athenians, centaurs and heroes; and scenes from the Panatheniac Festival. The temple's interior was dominated by another of Pheidias's statues, the *Athena Parthenos*, a colossal figure made of gold and ivory plates attached to a wooden framework.

Many types of craftsmen labored to make the Parthenon the supreme testament to their city's artistry. While building on the Acropolis continued, the workshops of Periclean Athens poured out objects whose quality was famous throughout the Greek world. Delicate jewelry, ornately painted pottery,

"Discus Thrower," by Myron, is among the great masterpieces of Greek art. It broke through a historic representational barrier by condensing a sequence of movements into a single pose without artificially freezing the action.

and gold drinking cups were traded from the Black Sea to the Strait of Gibraltar. All the arts had their charms, but few visitors to the city that would educate Greece could have left it without vivid memories of the works created by Athens's sculptors.

Abandoning the stiff, formalized style popular during the previous century, sculptors of Pericles' time had become adept in capturing the vitality and graceful proportions of the human body. Many of the great sculptors preferred to cast figures in bronze rather than to chisel marble because the metal allowed them more flexibility than the heavier stone. Always striving for the perfect form, they succeeded in creating gods who display a distinct semblance of humanity and humans who demonstrate a supernatural power. By combining their observations of the natural world with their visions of the

The dramatist Euripides depicted on a throne; the titles of his plays are inscribed in alphabetical order behind him. His tragedies are filled with dramatic acts of passion and examples of the flawed ideals that characterize human life.

ideal figure, Athenian artists were able to produce works with the delicate beauty of Pheidias's *Lemnian Athena* and the fluid strength of Myron's *Discus Thrower*.

Athenian artists were also famous for their wall paintings—none of which survive today, but traces can found in the delightful scenes that were painted on pottery using the red-figure decorative style. Against the black-painted backgrounds, the red figures of gods, men, animals, and monsters stand out boldly. Decorated funeral vases, mixing bowls, dishes, and oil jars — pieces intended for either ceremonial or everyday use — were exported by the Athenians, who had a monopoly on the production of painted pottery by the mid-5th century B.C. Designs often reflected the nature of the object they were painted on: Drinking cups and wine jars, for example, showed scenes of boisterous revelers and cavorting nymphs and satyrs. Displaying intimate details of the Athenians' fashions, sports, and customs, the paintings bring alive Pericles' city in all its lively intensity.

While some men used a brush or chisel to recreate the visions of their minds, others tried to capture in words the higher ideals that would give people a greater sense of moral purpose. Dramatists employed poetic images and lessons drawn from Greek myths to convey universal truths. Philosophers and scientists tried to find immutable laws and systems of reasoning that would help them to understand the world they lived in. Together, the Athenian thinkers left us with an impressive store of reflections on such topics as the horrors and glories of war, the nature of the ideal state and leader, and the duties of citizens to themselves and their city.

Our knowledge of Athenian tragedy rests mainly on the few remaining works of three much-honored dramatists. Aeschylus, the first of the great tragic poets, helped develop many of the technical innovations used on the early Athenian stage. In plays such as *Seven Against Thebes*, *Agamemnon*, and *Prometheus Bound*, Aeschylus dealt with the consequences of great crimes and how the world of gods and mortals was disrupted until the deeds were properly punished. The second of the tragedians was Sophocles, who produced such works as *Oedipus the King*, *Antigone*, and *Electra*. He believed that every person's life was ruled by a divinely decreed fate, and his work concerned the struggles of men and women to win vindication for their suffering. Euripides, the last of the trio, examined the effects on society of war, slavery, unjust laws, and the mistreatment of women and children. *Medea*, *The Trojan Women*, *Bacchae*, and Euripides' other tragedies are filled with vengeful murders, noble self-sacrifices, and other acts of passion that were reflections on the Athenians' world.

The tragedians presented the broad scope of the Athenians' inquiring spirit, but it was the comic poets who probably best captured the real essence of Pericles' city. Boldly sniping at public figures — such as the "onion- headed" leader of Athens — and mocking even the most honored social conventions,

> *There are many wonderful things, and nothing is more wonderful than man.*
> —SOPHOCLES
> Athenian dramatist
> in his play *Antigone*

The Athenian philosophical tradition culminated in the work of the 4th-century B.C. philosopher Aristotle. His resolution of early philosophers' abstractions with the world of the senses channeled Greek thought in the direction of scientific research.

the comic artist made his audience see the absurd rationales that often governed their actions. In the plays of the master comic poet Aristophanes, horrible puns, lewd jokes, and slapstick farce are combined with wildly fantastic plots to produce serious commentary on everyday affairs. Although the comedians held up Pericles' ideals to much ridicule, it is a testament to Athens's commitment to free speech that they were able to take liberties for which they would have been severely punished in any other state.

The Athenians also made names for themselves as orators, historians, and lyricists, but it was in the field of philosophy that they really excelled. The pursuit of truth and knowledge was a full-time occupation for men such as Socrates, who invented a method employing rigorous questioning of a person's beliefs to make the individual reexamine flaws in his thinking. Socrates had many students, among them Pericles' foster son Alcibiades and the

Ostracism ballots with the names of Themistocles, Cimon, Pericles, and others were found in excavations of the agora. The system of political exile, which was used to rid the Athenian government of unpopular citizens for 10 years at a time, derives its name from the pottery shards, *ostraka*, on which the undesirables' names were scratched.

master theorist Plato. The Athenian philosophical tradition culminated in the encyclopedic work of Aristotle in the 4th century B.C. Although in time many Athenian philosophers would come to be derided as sophists — quibblers and hairsplitters — they made important investigations into advanced systems of logic, codes of moral conduct, and the bases of natural laws.

The Golden Age of Athens was the work of artists, craftsmen, and writers of many fields attempting to glorify their city while at the same time inquiring into man's place in the universe. The true extent of their contributions to human learning can only be guessed at, but the Athenians clearly gave those who followed in their footsteps much to think about, much to admire, and much to imitate.

Spectacular as the achievements of Periclean Athens may seem today, not all of Pericles' contemporaries agreed with his civic-spending program. Some critics, especially among the aristocratic factions, believed that the tribute collected from Athens's allies should be used only to defend the Aegean, not to decorate the Acropolis or to employ the masses. Resenting the grand monuments of democratic Athens that were rising all around them, these discontented conservatives decided to use the public-spending issue in an all-out effort to drive Pericles from power.

The campaign against Pericles' administration was led by a famous wrestler and orator, the aris-

A fragment of a statuary horse exhibits great artistic energy and pride in craftsmanship characteristic of Athenian art of the Golden Age. Surviving literature and art from that period eloquently testify to the greatness of Athenian civilization.

tocrat Thucydides (not the historian of the same name). Under Thucydides the conservative factions were briefly united, standing and voting together in the assembly in an organized bloc. The conservative leader hoped to weaken Pericles' immense popular support by portraying him as a would-be tyrant and reckless waster of public funds.

Pericles was forced to defend his spending programs in front of the assembly. In a series of brilliant debates likened by commentators of the time to a match between two champion wrestlers, Pericles and Thucydides each strove to win the favorable opinion of the public. Pointing out the prosperity his programs had brought to the city, Pericles asked the Athenians if he had spent too much. "Far too much," they said. In that case, Pericles said, he would pay for the buildings himself, but the name inscribed on them would be his own, not that of the Athenian populace. He was bluffing, of course; his personal fortune was an iota of the cost of the works. But the Athenians understood Pericles' point: The Parthenon was the work not of a rich aristocrat but of the democratic citizens of Athens. To share in the glory they must share in the expenses. The Athenians were delighted by Pericles' sharp reply, and they told him to spend whatever he wanted from the public treasury. Pericles was thus able to beat back Thucydides' challenge. Many Athenians also believed that Thucydides' group was a threat to the democratic government, and in 443 B.C. they voted to ostracize the conservative leader. The Acropolis would get its fabulous marble and gold crown.

7

The Olympian

Pericles had deftly guided the Athenian ship of state through many storms, and for more than 10 years after Thucydides' exile no one would seriously challenge his right to direct the city's affairs. Even though he had wide public support, Pericles was not so much beloved as respected. He had proven himself as a great statesman, administrator, and general, but his complex and sometimes forbidding nature kept the people at a distance, in awe of the superior "Olympian." That was exactly how he wanted it.

Always reserved, businesslike, and immersed in state affairs, Pericles never attended any of the dinner parties and social gatherings that other men so enjoyed. The only street on which he could be met during the day was the one leading from his home to the agora and council chambers. He stayed out of the public eye, speaking before the assembly only on the most important occasions. Unlike many of the Athenian leaders who came after him, Pericles was not a demagogue, winning votes with fiery speeches against the people's favorite targets. He

There were all kinds of disorder to be found among a mass of citizens who possessed an empire as great as that of Athens, and Pericles was the only man capable of keeping each of these under control.
—PLUTARCH
Greek historian

The Periclean principle — that every Athenian citizen was entitled, even obligated, to participate in his city's affairs — brought Athens a degree of democracy unparalleled by any other culture of the age.

A 19th-century drawing depicts Pericles speaking to a group of Athenians. Renowned for his oratory, he spoke in public only on important occasions and earned respect by supporting policies that were wise rather than simply popular.

supported policies that he believed were right for Athens, not just those he knew would be popular. Because he was esteemed by his fellow generals and the council members, he usually had little trouble finding men who would fight hard for his programs.

Pericles had succeeded in bringing to Athens a degree of democracy unknown in any other city. Every citizen could serve Athens — whether as a general, jury member, or soldier — and be paid for the work. Even the aristocrats, men who still firmly believed that people of good birth and education were better able to govern than were shopkeepers and merchants, accepted Pericles' principle that every Athenian citizen was entitled, even obligated, to participate in the city's affairs.

The conservatives' resistance to Pericles' programs was largely muted after Thucydides was ostracized. What opposition Pericles did face over the next dozen years came increasingly from ambitious new leaders of the more radical democratic factions. These men, many of whom had formerly hawked sausages or run tanneries, had seized advantage of the opportunities that had recently opened up for them in Athens's government. They now sought issues to challenge Pericles' ruling coalition, which they considered to be too aristocratic. Generally, however, Pericles was able to satisfy all segments of Athenian society with policies designed to promote justice and increase prosperity.

Contentment at home was all very well, but the leader of imperial Athens also had to ensure that the city's allies were treated fairly. Following the peace in 445 B.C., Pericles began to reorganize Athens's tribute-collecting system. Some allies had stopped paying altogether, and others complained that their share was too high. With the tragedian Sophocles heading the board that established the new tribute lists, the problems in the empire's financial system were ironed out. Many of the allies were given sharply reduced assessments.

Pericles further strengthened the empire by establishing colonies throughout the Aegean. Some were set up on land belonging to allies of Athens, in which case those states' tribute was reduced as compensation. Groups of colonists were also sent to strategic spots along the coast of Thrace, the region in the northern Aegean that included northeastern Greece, to establish trading posts in an area rich in timber and silver mines. The new colonies helped to keep less trustworthy allies in line, extended Athens's influence into regions with vital natural resources, and allowed the city to drain off some of its excess population. The colonists were loyal Athenian citizens who were given incentives of cheap land and low taxes so that they would settle in distant areas and protect the empire's borders.

Despite Pericles' efforts to maintain peace within the empire, disputes between Athens's allies sometimes arose. A conflict between Miletus, a seaport

We do not say that a man who takes no interest in politics is a man who minds his own business, we say that he has no business here at all.
—PERICLES

85

ΚΗΦΙΣΟΦΩΝΓΑΙΑΝΙΕΥΣ
ΕΓΡΑΜΜΑΤΕΥΕ
ΑΜΙΟΙ Ο ΟΙΜΕ ΤΑ ΤΟ ΔΙ ΜΟ ΤΟ ΑΘΗΝΑΙ
ΠΝΕΓΕΝΟΝΤΟ

The goddesses Athena and Hera were depicted together on a plaque commemorating a treaty between Athens and the island of Samos, which had rebelled against Athenian domination in 440 B.C.

on Asia Minor, and the island of Samos in 440 B.C. grew into a full-scale rebellion when the powerful Samians refused to allow Athens to resolve the matter through arbitration. Pericles at once led a fleet against Samos and replaced the oligarchic regime there with a democratic government. After Pericles left, however, the Samian oligarchs regained control, revolted against Athens, and appealed to Sparta and its allies for help. Seeing that the empire was once again in danger, Pericles gathered a large naval force and descended on Samos. This time the sides seemed more evenly matched; Pericles won two naval battles, but an Athenian army was defeated on land. Finally, after a nine-month siege, Samos surrendered. Pericles tore down the Samians' walls, stripped them of their fleet, and imposed a heavy fine on them, but in general the terms of surrender were not particularly harsh.

When Pericles returned home he gave a funeral oration mourning the Athenian lives lost at Samos, saying, "It seems to us that the spring has gone out of the year." But the suppression of the revolt had greatly strengthened Athens's imperial authority, and the Athenians were now even more attentive to their allies' complaints. In addition, Sparta and the other members of the Peloponnesian League made no attempt to interfere in the Samian conflict. The terms of the Thirty Years' Peace were being obeyed.

The Samians were not the only ones who tried to cut their ties with the Athenians during 440–439 B.C. Athens's access to the Black Sea region had been threatened by the rebellion of Byzantium, a city located on the site of present-day Istanbul, on the Bosporus waterway leading into the sea. Pericles had brought Byzantium back into the fold bloodlessly, but he knew that further efforts were needed to secure Athens's trade routes to its most important source of fish and grain. In 437 B.C. Pericles commanded a fleet that sailed to areas throughout the Black Sea, establishing colonies and opening relations with local rulers.

Back home again, the busy general had time to pursue personal relationships. For most of his life Pericles, like most other Athenian men interested in cultural matters, had probably spent his leisure time with a group of male associates discussing the issues of the day. Women were not expected to have any intellectual interests. But Pericles' outlook on women was greatly broadened after he met the beautiful, witty, and intelligent Aspasia. Born on Miletus, this famous courtesan had moved to Athens, where she entertained and educated Athens's leading men. Whether or not Pericles married Aspasia is uncertain, but he did fall deeply in love with her.

> *We cannot see the gods, but we believe them to be immortal from the honors we pay them and the blessings we receive from them, so it is with those who have given their lives for their country.*
> —PERICLES
> in a funeral oration for Athenian soldiers who died during the revolt of Samos

The two worked well together: Aspasia's advice on state affairs and speech writing was highly valued by Pericles. They had one son, who was also called Pericles.

Some Athenians were appalled that a woman — and a foreign-born prostitute, to boot — had gained such an influential position in city affairs. Brought to trial on a charge of impiety (not showing proper reverence to the gods), Aspasia escaped conviction, it is told, only after Pericles himself pled for her in front of the jury. Pericles' enemies next used the impiety accusation against his longtime counselor Anaxagoras, who had supposedly committed a sacrilege by proposing that worldly events were governed by natural causes. The old philosopher had to flee from Athens. Even the sculptor Pheidias was forced into exile. He was proved innocent of embezzling gold adorning the statue of Athena Parthenos because Pericles, knowing that such a charge would at some point be made, had ordered that all gold

The opponents of Pericles used his love affair with the famous courtesan Aspasia (pictured) to attack him. Aspasia's influence was greatly resented in a society where women traditionally exercised little influence.

A panel relief from the Acropolis shows Athena in a mournful pose. The first signals that war between Greece's two greatest powers was imminent appeared in 435 B.C. when Corinth threatened to upset the balance of power between the Delian and Peloponnesian leagues.

used on the figure be attached in removable sheets so that it could be weighed and compared against official accounts. Pheidias was, however, found guilty of including his and Pericles' likenesses on Athena's shield.

With no way of attacking Pericles personally, his opponents could only try to harass his friends instead. One attempt was made to have Pericles himself charged with stealing temple funds and tried before the altar of the god Apollo, but Pericles easily blocked the suit. The Athenians agreed that Pericles

A contemporary photograph shows the ancient citadel of Corcyra on the island of Corfu. Athens's decision to help protect Corcyra from Corinthian takeover led to the end of peaceful relations between the Peloponnesian League and the Athenian Empire.

was quite liberal with his use of funds for building projects, but they also knew that he was incorruptible and totally devoted to his city. To dispel the notion that he intended to become dictator, Pericles was careful not to misuse his powers and was tolerant of even the most abusive criticism hurled at him. The attacks, he believed, were normal signs of healthy debate in a democratic society. He, in turn, felt free to bluntly reprimand the Athenians when he thought that they were being irresponsible.

The low level of public bickering reflected the relatively peaceful conditions elsewhere in Greece during 445–435 B.C. The Athenians and the Spartans had maintained the terms of their treaty. They had avoided serious confrontations, and the friendship between King Archidamus and Pericles had been a

key factor. The Peloponnesian states had even accepted Pericles' invitation to join Athens in founding a colony amid the thriving Greek cities on the Italian peninsula. The original colonists in the panhellenic settlement of Thurii included such luminaries as the historian Herodotus and the city planner Hippodamus, who designed Thurii according to a grid system, with straight streets and specially zoned commercial and residential districts. Athens and the other Greek cities usually had quite irregular layouts.

It was in the west, however, that the first dark clouds appeared to signal the coming of a cataclysmic civil war in Greece. The trade route to the rich Italian markets was of major importance to Corinth — much more so than for Athens. In 435 B.C. Corinth became involved in a dispute with one of its

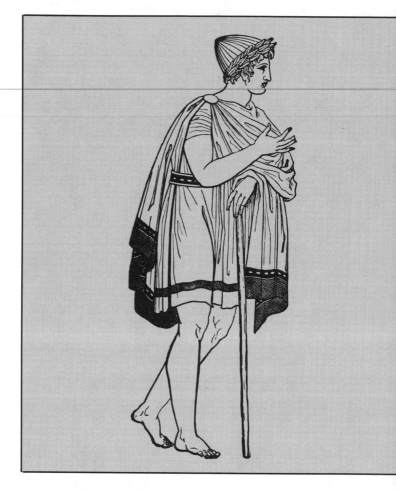

Athenian citizens typically wore a *chiton* (undergarment) and *chlamys* (a short, draped mantle) secured at the shoulder by a *fibulum*, as shown on the left. Men wore a loose, draped outergarment similar to a toga when appearing formally in public, as shown on the right.

old colonies, Corcyra (modern-day Corfu), an island in the Ionian Sea. When Corcyra, the third largest Greek naval power, refused to agree to its mother-city's demands, war broke out. Corcyra won an initial encounter, but feared that the Corinthians would follow up with a massive attack. The Corcyreans therefore appealed to Athens for help, although the two states were bound by no treaty of alliance.

Pericles did not want a conflict with Corinth, for that would almost certainly lead to war with Sparta. He could not, however, allow Corinth to capture the Corcyrean navy and shift the balance of power decisively in favor of the Peloponnesian League. After lengthy discussions, the Athenian assembly agreed

to a defensive pact with Corcyra and sent a small fleet to help protect the island.

The Corinthians were enraged. Assembling a large flotilla of ships with the help of its Peloponnesian allies, Corinth set out to conquer Corcyra. In a great battle off the nearby island of Sybota, the Corcyrean-Athenian fleet was overwhelmed. The surviving ships gathered for a last stand off Corcyra. But just as the Corinthians were about to complete their triumph, they spotted a new Athenian fleet approaching. Reinforcements sent by Pericles had arrived at an opportune moment. Unwilling to risk a more serious encounter with Athens, the frustrated Corinthians sailed homeward, swearing they would gain vengeance.

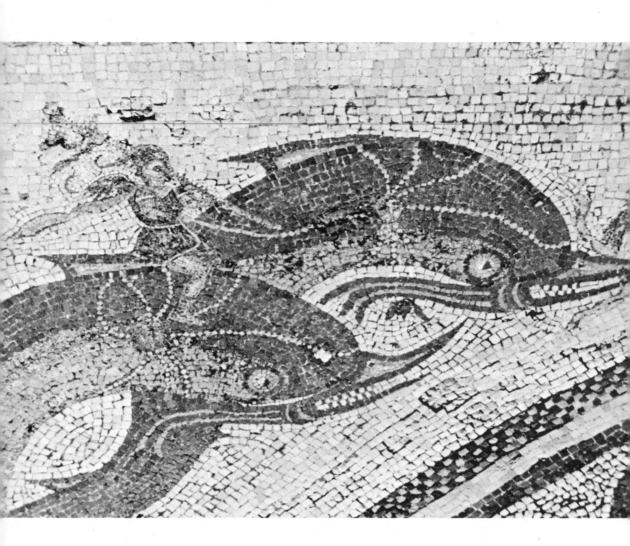

A whimsical mosaic of dolphins in harness from the island of Delos, headquarters of the Delian League. The league was formed in 477 B.C. as a confederation of Greek states with Athens as its head. As Athens developed its empire, its allies in the league were reduced to virtual vassal states.

The Battle of Sybota signaled the end of the peaceful relations between the Peloponnesian League and the Athenian Empire. As Corinth continued its attacks on unfriendly states in western Greece, Pericles decided that certain steps must be taken to prepare Athens for the conflict looming ahead. First, a larger portion of Athens's budget was set aside for the city's defense. Pericles then slapped a crippling trade embargo on the neighboring state of Megara, which supported Corinth against Corcyra but depended heavily on its commercial ties with the Athenian Empire. Finally, troops were sent to the northwestern Aegean to establish a stronger Athenian presence in a region dominated by the kingdoms of Thrace and Macedon. The campaigns there were expensive, because Athens had to move against an ally, the city of Potidaea, which refused to obey an Athenian order to tear down its walls. Potidaea, a Corinthian colony, did not surrender until 430 B.C., after a difficult two-year siege.

Tensions between the chief Greek cities had been stretched to the snapping point. Corinth was stirring up trouble for Athens everywhere, and many of the Spartans had begun to believe that Pericles was deliberately trying to provoke a war. In the summer of 432 B.C. the Spartan council invited delegates from the Peloponnesian League cities and other states to come and air their grievances against Athens. The Megarians complained bitterly about the trade embargo. The Aeginetans cried that Athens had reduced them to little more than slaves. The Corinthians painted Athens as blackly as possible, trying to prove that the Athenians were intent on ruling the whole of Greece. Only the Athenian ambassadors in Sparta had anything good to say about their city, and they warned the Spartans to think hard before bringing on a war that promised huge costs and few rewards.

The Spartan council voted; a majority of the members believed that Athens had broken the treaty signed in the winter of 446–445 B.C. The Thirty Years' Peace had lasted for less than 14. Greece prepared for war.

8

The Perils of War

Historians throughout the ages have debated whether or not the Peloponnesian War was inevitable. The conflict, which began in 431 B.C. and continued with intermittent breaks for 27 years, has aroused such attention largely for two reasons. First, the war ended the Golden Age of Greece. Second, the 5th-century B.C. Athenian historian Thucydides, the first man to attempt a thorough investigation into the causes of a war, chose this conflict for his subject.

In his great work, *History of the Peloponnesian War*, Thucydides recorded many of the factors that bred hostility between the Greek cities, but he asserted that the principal cause of the war was the Spartans' fear of the large Athenian Empire. The war, he believed, would have broken out sooner or later and was not, as some contemporary chroniclers have written, caused by Pericles' supposed desire for a showdown with Sparta. Modern-day historians have given many different explanations for the war, and some think that the war could have been avoided but for fatal misjudgments by the leaders of the rival states.

[The Greek statesmen] all failed to foresee the evil consequences that [the Peloponnesian War] would have for everyone, victors and vanquished alike, that it would bring economic ruin, class warfare, brutality, erosion of moral standards, and a permanent instability that left Greece vulnerable to foreign conquest.
—DONALD KAGAN
American historian

The ruins of the temple of Zeus in Athens. At the outset of the Peloponnesian War, Sparta attempted to discredit Pericles by challenging his religious convictions. Many Athenians lost faith in their gods as the devastations of war and a lethal plague set in.

A bust of Thucydides, the great historian whose *History of the Peloponnesian War* was the first attempt by a historian to analyze the causes of a war. He believed that the Spartans' fear of the expanding Athenian Empire was largely responsible for the conflict.

Pericles firmly believed that it was the Spartans who had miscalculated; Athens, he stated, was merely protecting its interests. It had not sought to expand its empire, nor had it attacked any of Sparta's allies. Nonetheless, war had been declared, and Pericles told the Athenians to prepare themselves.

The military shipyards at Piraeus became busy once again. The Long Walls were checked for weak points. An accounting was taken of the gold talents stored in the Athenian treasury. Athens was going to meet the Spartan challenge with its chief assets: its navy, its defensive fortifications, and its money.

Hostilities did not begin until a half year after the Spartan declaration of war. There were many in both Sparta and Athens who questioned the wisdom of going to war, and during the intervening months three Spartan embassies delivered ultimatums that the Athenians must agree to if they wanted peace. On the first occasion the Spartans demanded that Athens "drive out the curse of the goddess," an attack on Pericles, whose mother's family, the Alcmaeonids, had committed a sacrilege against Athena two centuries before. Sparta was hoping to divide the Athenians against their leader, especially those who questioned Pericles' religious devoutness. The move backfired, however; the Athenians rallied behind Pericles and countered with their own demands, stating that Sparta must expel all those connected with two curses of its own.

The demands of the second Spartan embassy were harder for Pericles to reject. Sparta's main requirement was that Athens end its economic embargo of Megara. To many Athenians the new terms did not seem unreasonable, and the proposal was hotly debated in the assembly. Finally, Pericles stepped onto

Athens's *triremes*, so called for their three banks of oars, provided the major offensive and defensive elements in Pericles' strategy against Sparta, which was designed to avoid direct encounters with the Spartan army.

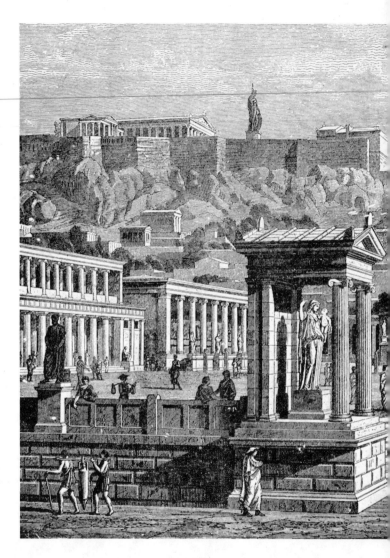

The agora of Athens, with the Acropolis and Athena Promachos in the background. Famine, plague, and the casualties of war reduced the greatest city civilization had produced to a giant cemetery in 430 B.C.

the podium. "Athenians," he began, "my views are the same as ever. I am against making any concessions to the Peloponnesians." Sparta was determined to humble Athens, he warned, and if they gave in on the matter of Megara the Spartans would only make further demands. If Sparta was really interested in peace, it would submit the dispute to arbitration, as the treaty between the two states dictated.

The assembly was persuaded by Pericles' speech and voted to reject the second Spartan ultimatum,

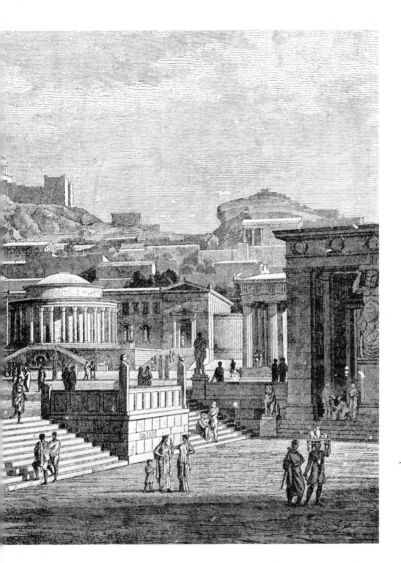

thereby ending any hope of avoiding a war. An Athenian offer to hold discussions about the points of dispute brought no reply from the Spartans. By the time the third Spartan embassy reached Attica, bearing the clearly unacceptable demand that Athens "give the Greeks their freedom" — relinquish its empire — an army was already marching out of the Peloponnesus.

Pericles had not wanted a war; he may simply have underestimated the resentment that other Greek cities felt toward Athens. Proud as always of his city's power, and seeing no reason to apologize for it, he refused to back down before any challenge. And yet, if his city had to fight, this was a good time for it to go to war. Athens's navy controlled the seas, its empire was strong and united, its war treasury was enormous — and Pericles, though about 60 years old, could still provide effective wartime leadership.

The Athenian war strategy as mapped out by Pericles seemed bound to succeed. Athens would avoid encounters with the main Spartan army. Sitting safely behind their city's walls, supplied by their imperial domains, the Athenians would send out fleets to scourge the Peloponnesian coastline. Sparta's agrarian economy could not support a long war, and its army would be frustrated by a foe that refused to fight major battles and yet struck elsewhere at will. Unlike the Athenian Empire, the Peloponnesian League was a loosely knit organization that would surely fall apart under the strains of war.

Avoiding unnecessary risks was the key to winning the war, Pericles believed. Would the overconfident Athenians be hurt while attempting too much at once, as had happened in the past? Or, on the other hand, would bold initiatives again reap huge rewards? In the spring of 431 B.C. the fighting that would bring answers to these questions finally broke out.

The war's initial engagement took place in Boeotia. Thebes tried to seize Athens's ally Plataea but was repulsed. The attack on the city triggered calls for the mustering of armies throughout Greece. Sparta was supported by most of the states on the mainland; Athens by the cities on the islands. Assembling the Peloponnesian forces, King Archidamus marched toward Attica. As soon as news of the Spartan approach reached him, Pericles requested that all those living in the Attic countryside gather their possessions and take refuge inside Athens's walls. Fearing that the Spartan council would shrewdly try to damage his political standing by ordering his friend Archidamus to spare his property, Pericles turned all his landholdings over to Athens.

The first summer of the war severely tested the Athenian resolve. Archidamus sat still for a while, hoping that the Athenians would ask for peace. But when the grain was high in midsummer, the Spartans began their campaign through Attica and set the fields north of Athens aflame. The mood in Athens was ugly. Refugees had crowded into the city and had set up tents and shacks on every plot of free land from Piraeus to the northern walls. As more and more farms near Athens went up in smoke, Pericles found it increasingly difficult to avoid a clash with the Spartan Army.

Although it was probably of little consolation to the farmers whose crops were destroyed, Pericles made sure that the Peloponnesian states were repaid for their work in Attica. All that summer an Athenian fleet attacked points along the peninsula's coastline, burning down farms and capturing many towns. In the fall the main Athenian army linked up with the fleet at the Isthmus of Corinth to ravage the countryside around Megara. The Spartans eventually marched home, the Athenian forces went back to their bases in Attica, and at the end of the year Pericles gave his famous funeral oration.

The second year of the war began, and again Archidamus returned with his army to devastate the Athenian lands from end to end. This time, however, the Spartans left Attica earlier than they intended, in an almost fearful manner. It was not Athens's army that the Spartans were afraid of, however; something far more deadly had made itself at home in the city.

The Piraeus docks — from which Athens's fleets ventured out on raiding expeditions and into which grain shipments for the hungry populace flowed — also exposed the city to dangerous attacks from abroad. In the summer of 430 B.C. ships arrived at Piraeus bearing an unseen invader from Ethiopia, a singularly lethal plague. In the crowded, unhealthy refugee quarters of wartime Athens, the contagious sickness spread with horrifying speed. By midsummer Greece's greatest city had become a giant cemetery.

> *We must not cry over the loss of houses and land but of men's lives; since houses and land do not gain men, but men them.*
> —PERICLES
> on why the war with Sparta needed to continue

The plague's victims suffered a variety of ailments, including burning sensations, fits of coughing, fever, pustules on the skin, and delirium. Nothing that the Athenian doctors or priests tried against the sickness was of any use. The temples and other public buildings filled with bodies, and the dead were burned or buried in haphazard fashion without the usual ceremonies. Law and order broke down; in the face of the great indiscriminate death, no one had any fear of punishment. Because prayers for relief from the plague went unanswered, few people continued to worship the gods. Many people spent all their money on immediate pleasures, expecting to be dead before long.

Pericles was away from Athens during the height of the plague. To distract the Athenians from Archidamus's second invasion of Attica, Pericles had led another huge naval expedition to the Peloponnesus in early summer. His fleet damaged a number of enemy strongholds, but when Pericles docked again in Piraeus he found his city in horrible agony. Their countryside burned, their streets littered with the dead and dying, their army in the midst of losing one quarter of its men to the plague, their temples deserted by the gods, the Athenians' morale was very low. A scapegoat was needed, and none was better suited for the role than the man who had urged his fellow citizens to go to war. Many Athenians bitterly attacked Pericles' policies, and the assembly voted to send a peace embassy to Sparta.

Knowing how terribly his people were suffering, Pericles tried to comfort them, reason with them, and give them the courage to carry on. He defended the earlier decision to reject the Spartans' demands and pointed out how powerful Athens remained. His war strategy had been sound, he insisted; the only peril he had not foreseen was the plague. Some of his words sank in. But although the Athenians agreed to continue the war, they no longer wanted Pericles to lead them. They deposed him from office and fined him heavily for not maintaining accurate treasury records during the disorders caused by the plague.

> *The most terrible thing of all was the despair into which people fell when they realized they had caught the plague; . . . Terrible too was the sight of people dying like sheep as a result of nursing others.*
> —THUCYDIDES
> Athenian historian

Dispirited, Pericles shut himself up at home, abandoning the political arena that had been the center of his life. The last year had been extremely hard on him. The plague had killed many close friends and most of his relatives. Among the dead was his eldest son, Xanthippus. When his second son, Paralus, also fell sick and died, Pericles was completely devastated. For the first time, the cool, detached Athenian leader let down his guard and sobbed uncontrollably as he laid a wreath on his son's body.

The Athenians did not allow Pericles to sit grieving for long. Dissatisfied with the inexperienced leaders who tried to replace Pericles, the people recalled him to service and apologized for their previous treatment of him. Although weary and

A mosaic portrait of Alexander the Great of Macedon. The great Athenian Empire had been destroyed by 400 B.C. Alexander built a vast, international Greek empire three generations later, but his death in 323 B.C. marked the end of the great Hellenic age.

heartsick, he resumed his old position on the board of generals to direct the war effort. In the midst of the third year's fighting, Pericles asked the assembly for a favor. His eldest sons were dead and he had no heir: Would the Athenians grant citizenship to his son by Aspasia so that the boy could bear the family name? Despite the law that Pericles himself had passed forbidding citizenship to anyone whose parents were not both Athenian, the assembly voted to ignore the statute for the younger Pericles.

With the inheritance problem resolved, Pericles could die with some peace of mind. In the autumn of 429 B.C. he caught the plague and gradually lost all his strength. As he lay on his deathbed listening to his friends talk about his great deeds, Pericles broke in on the discussion to state what he believed was his supreme achievement: "No Athenian ever put on mourning because of me." By this he meant that he had never misused his power to harm his opponents, and no disasters had ever befallen Athens through any mistakes of his. Pericles died knowing that he had led his city well.

The Periclean Age had ended, and within a quarter century the Athenian Empire was destroyed. The leaders who followed Pericles frittered away Athens's strength, mistreating the city's allies and engaging in foolish military expeditions. Foremost among these men was Pericles' foster son, Alcibiades, a brilliant war commander but an unscrupulous political intriguer who made a mockery of Pericles' high ideals. The biggest loser in the Peloponnesian War was not Athens but the whole of Greece, which was exhausted by the conflict and the continuing battles for supremacy in the decades that followed. Finally, in 339 B.C., King Philip of Macedon won control of Greece. His son, Alexander the Great, led a Greek army against the Persian Empire and conquered it in only four years. When Alexander died in Babylon in 323 B.C., the influence of Greek civilization had been spread as far eastward as India. But the Greek states would henceforth be dominated by larger powers, first by the competing sections that split from Alexander's empire, and later by Rome.

He considered it the highest of all his claims to honor that, despite the immense power he wielded, he had never given way to feelings of envy and hatred and had treated no man as so irreconcilable an enemy that he could never become a friend.

—PLUTARCH
Greek historian

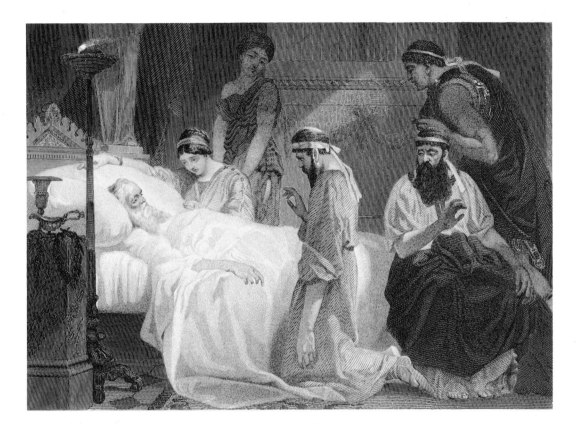

Today, Pericles is remembered as the guiding light of the city where democratic traditions first reached maturity and where a culture flourished that could produce artists and thinkers of the stature of Socrates, Pheidias, and Euripides. Pericles believed that men and women were great works in themselves and that the duty of the state was to respect each individual so that every citizen in turn could respect the state. As Athens's leader, he insisted that power should never be used merely to gain more power, that behind every great ambition there must be a greater aim. His words remind us of the infinite heights that can be achieved through people of vision and noble spirit. Monuments crumble, empires fall, names are forgotten, but great ideals live on in the minds of later generations. Like the spear point of *Athena Promachos* guiding voyagers to their destination, the glory of Pericles' city still shines out to us from long ago and far away.

A neoclassical engraving of the death of Pericles. The plague that killed his two sons, his closest friends, and countless Athenian citizens claimed the life of Pericles as well. His life remains a model of the infinite heights attainable by those of vision and noble spirit.

Further Reading

Bowra, C. M. *Periclean Athens.* New York: Dial Press, 1971.

Burn, A. R. *Pericles and Athens.* New York: Macmillan, 1943.

Herodotus. *The Persian Wars.* Translated by George Rawlinson. New York: Random House, 1964.

Hooper, Finley. *Greek Realities.* Detroit: Wayne State University Press, 1978.

Kagan, Donald. *The Outbreak of the Peloponnesian War.* Ithaca, NY: Cornell University Press, 1969.

Plutarch. *The Rise and Fall of Athens.* Translated by Ian Scott-Kilvert. New York: Viking Penguin, 1960.

Sutcliff, Rosemary. *The Flowers of Adonis.* New York: Coward-McCann, 1969.

Thucydides. *The Peloponnesian War.* Translated by Rex Warner. New York: Viking Penguin, 1954.

Warner, Rex. *Men of Athens.* New York: Viking Press, 1972.

Chronology

ca. 493 B.C.	Pericles born
490	Athenians rout Persian army at Battle of Marathon
480	Xerxes invades Greece and burns Athens; Themistocles leads Greece to victory at Salamis
477	Athens forms alliance of Greek Aegean states known as Delian League
472	Pericles sponsors original presentation of Aeschylus' play *The Persians*
470	Athenians ostracize Themistocles
469	Cimon leads Greeks to victory over Persians at Eurydemon River
463–461	Ephialtes and Pericles lead successful political campaign against conservative Council of Areopagus, opening the way for democratic reforms in Athens Athenians ostracize Cimon
458	Sparta gains narrow victory over Athens at Battle of Tanagra; Athens wins control of Aegina and much of central Greece
454	Delian League treasury moved to Athens; Pericles elected general
451	Pericles sends Cimon to negotiate a five years' truce with Sparta
449	Athens signs peace treaty with Persia; Pericles begins program to rebuild temples and public structures destroyed by Xerxes
446–445	Pericles commands Athens's defense of its empire against Spartan-backed rebellion; concludes peace treaty with Sparta
440–439	Suppresses revolt on Samos
437	Leads naval expedition to Black Sea
435	Athens forms alliance with Corcyra against Corinth
431	Peloponnesian War breaks out between Athenian and Spartan alliances; Pericles delivers funeral oration
430	Plague ravages Athens during second year of war
429	Pericles dies in Athens

Index

Perry Scott King is an editor at Chelsea House and a student of ancient civilizations. A graduate of Drew University, he lives with his wife, the writer Susan Gilbert, in Brooklyn.

Arthur M. Schlesinger, jr., taught history at Harvard for many years and is currently Albert Schweitzer Professor of the Humanities at City University of New York. He is the author of numerous highly praised works in American history and has twice been awarded the Pulitzer Prize. He served in the White House as special assistant to Presidents Kennedy and Johnson.

MAKERS OF THE MIDDLE AGES AND RENAISSANCE

Chaucer

Celebrated Poet and Author

Chaucer
Celebrated Poet and Author

Janet Hubbard-Brown

CHELSEA HOUSE
PUBLISHERS
A Haights Cross Communications Company ®
Philadelphia

COVER: Portrait of Geoffrey Chaucer. c. 1590.

CHELSEA HOUSE PUBLISHERS
VP, NEW PRODUCT DEVELOPMENT Sally Cheney
DIRECTOR OF PRODUCTION Kim Shinners
CREATIVE MANAGER Takeshi Takahashi
MANUFACTURING MANAGER Diann Grasse

Staff for Chaucer
EXECUTIVE EDITOR Lee Marcott
EDITORIAL ASSISTANT Carla Greenberg
PRODUCTION EDITOR Noelle Nardone
COVER AND INTERIOR DESIGNER Keith Trego
LAYOUT 21st Century Publishing and Communications, Inc.

A Haights Cross Communications ✦ Company ®

www.chelseahouse.com

First Printing

9 8 7 6 5 4 3 2 1

Library of Congress Cataloging-in-Publication Data

Hubbard-Brown, Janet
    Chaucer: celebrated poet and author/Janet Hubbard Brown
        p. cm.—(Makers of the Middle Ages and Renaissance)
    Includes bibliographical references and index.
    ISBN 0-7910-8635-6 (hardcover)
    1. Chaucer, Geoffrey, d. 1400—Juvenile literature. 2. Poets, English—
Middle English, 1100–1500—Biography—Juvenile literature. I. Title
II. Series.
PR1905.H76 2005
821'.1–dc22
                                                    2005004784

CONTENTS

Chaucer the Celebrated Poet

The year was 1387 and Geoffrey Chaucer sat down to write about a group of people making a pilgrimage to the Canterbury Cathedral in England. A pilgrimage was supposed to be a religious journey to pay homage to a saint. In the late medieval era in England, however, it was considered frivolous to take a vacation.

So, the pilgrimage was the perfect solution. Travelers could set out in the spring to walk on foot to Canterbury and other shrines, meet fellow voyagers, and enjoy the countryside at the same time. Chaucer was 57 years old and already famous among the members of the aristocracy in England who had heard him recite his poems and stories. If we believe the description he provides of himself in his stories—and we have no reason not to—he was a tall man who was probably overweight, with a large appetite for food, storytelling, and life.

Chaucer's goal with *The Canterbury Tales* was to create 120 stories to be told by 30 pilgrims. Of the 24 characters he did manage to put down on paper, several rank among the greatest literary figures of all time. One of those was Dame Alice, the Wife of Bath. Her character was based on a real woman named Alice Perrers, who was the mistress to King Edward III after his wife died. She was a larger-than-life woman who ended up being kicked out of the king's court by Parliament after she was caught stealing from the royal treasury. Chaucer and Alice Perrers were friends, however, and the portrait he painted of her expressed his admiration for her.

The characters in Geoffrey Chaucer's *The Canterbury Tales* are all on their way to a pilgrimage at Canterbury Cathedral in England. Each of the 24 characters acts as people would act in everyday life.

Dame Alice spoke her mind. She was a woman who always followed the rule of experience rather than authority. She told her listeners that she had five husbands, all of whom were now dead, and she claimed that experience made her an expert. She went on to tell stories about her former husbands, informing her listeners about how she was able to gain power over all of them.

The most humorous part of her tale dealt with her fourth husband, who, once they had married, spent all his time reading. All of the reading material, however, stressed how horrible women were. Dame Alice got sick of that and grabbed the book. She hit her husband so hard, he fell into the fire. Angry, he jumped up and hit her with his fist. She pretended to be dead. As soon as he came closer to check on her, she hit him again and then pretended to die once again. He became frightened. He promised her that, if she lived, he would give her complete mastery over him. She, of course, accepted the offer.[1]

Instead of having his pilgrims take turns telling stories, Chaucer wrote a drama in which people behaved the way they do in real life. Some of the tales were earthy folk tales, and the language was vulgar—a little shocking, even for modern readers. It is hard to imagine that a writer living in the fourteenth century could write stories that would not be considered suitable for a young adult audience today, but such was the case with *The Canterbury Tales.* A lot of swearing went on in those years, especially among the rich. "One gets the impression that Chaucer cussed a blue streak throughout the 1370s."[2]

Geoffrey Chaucer can be thought of as the world's first short-story writer, and all of his tales represent a different aspect of himself. There was the Chaucer who supported women, the literary Chaucer, the Chaucer who wrote about social events, the gloomy Chaucer, and the funny Chaucer. Chaucer achieved something else that had never been done before—he created characters that were boastful, nasty, foolish, and funny. He developed the art of satire, making fun of people in a literary way. He also developed a form of rhyming that worked so well that William Shakespeare, among many others, adopted it hundreds of years later.

The life of the author was as fascinating as the stories he told. Over a 60-year period, Chaucer served three kings, lived through a time of war, and survived plagues and many political and social upheavals. *The Canterbury Tales,* as much as they were

Today, Geoffrey Chaucer (shown here) can be thought of as the world's first short-story writer. Each of the stories in *The Canterbury Tales* represents an aspect of Chaucer's personality.

entertaining, were also a reflection of life in late medieval England. We learn, from a man writing in the fourteenth century, that people then were not very different than they are today. Their application to modern-day situations is what makes *The Canterbury Tales* so special. Before Chaucer wrote *The Canterbury Tales*, which are generally credited as the beginning of English literature, he also wrote many other poems and stories that are also worthy of recognition.

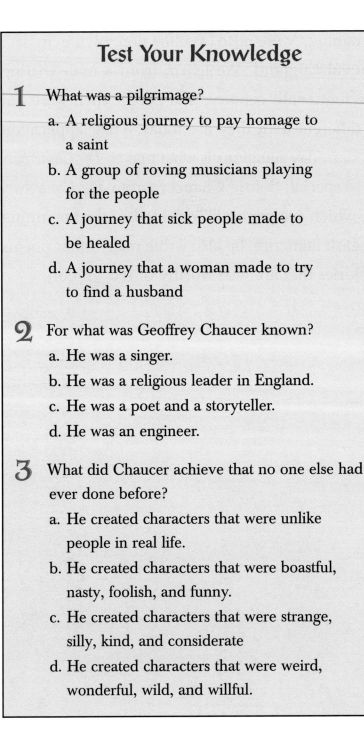

Test Your Knowledge

1 What was a pilgrimage?

   a. A religious journey to pay homage to a saint

   b. A group of roving musicians playing for the people

   c. A journey that sick people made to be healed

   d. A journey that a woman made to try to find a husband

2 For what was Geoffrey Chaucer known?

   a. He was a singer.

   b. He was a religious leader in England.

   c. He was a poet and a storyteller.

   d. He was an engineer.

3 What did Chaucer achieve that no one else had ever done before?

   a. He created characters that were unlike people in real life.

   b. He created characters that were boastful, nasty, foolish, and funny.

   c. He created characters that were strange, silly, kind, and considerate

   d. He created characters that were weird, wonderful, wild, and willful.

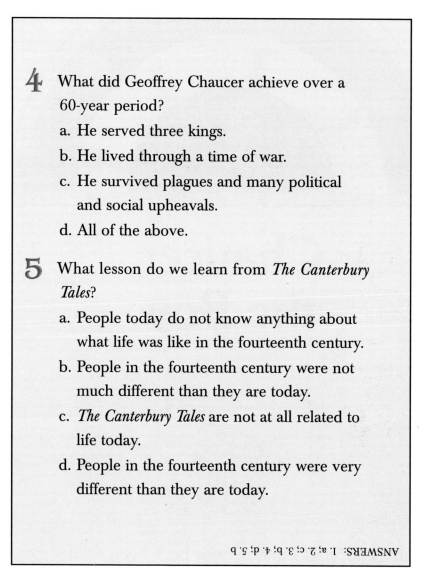

4 What did Geoffrey Chaucer achieve over a 60-year period?

a. He served three kings.

b. He lived through a time of war.

c. He survived plagues and many political and social upheavals.

d. All of the above.

5 What lesson do we learn from *The Canterbury Tales*?

a. People today do not know anything about what life was like in the fourteenth century.

b. People in the fourteenth century were not much different than they are today.

c. *The Canterbury Tales* are not at all related to life today.

d. People in the fourteenth century were very different than they are today.

ANSWERS: 1. a; 2. c; 3. b; 4. d; 5. b

Chaucer the Boy

J ohn Chaucer of London must have been excited, just as any man would be today, to learn that he would be the father of a baby boy. When his son Geoffrey was born, sometime between 1340 and 1344, John Chaucer was a wealthy man who had married well and was prepared to raise a family. During the 1340s, childbirth and child care were much more dangerous than they are today, so newborns were christened immediately. It was believed that this was the only way for them to enter heaven. The ritual of baptism was a sign that the baby was part of the Christian faith. It also announced that the child was being brought into society. The Catholic Church was firmly established in England during the Middle Ages. People basically had two rulers. Their souls were under the care of the pope, who was in Rome, but was represented by his bishops and priests. Their physical well-being was under the protection of the king, who, at the time of Geoffrey Chaucer's birth, was King Edward III.

John Chaucer and his wife, Agnes de Copton, would have already selected godparents for their baby before he was born—two people of the same gender as the child and one of the opposite gender. A great deal of thought went into the selections. The godparents were expected to play a strong role in the religious instruction of the child. During the ceremony, the child was given a name. It was common to name the child after the principal godparent of the same gender. The most popular

The physical well-being of the people of England was entrusted to the king. At the time of Geoffrey Chaucer's birth, King Edward III ruled England. The king is shown here on his throne, dressed in a tunic with English and French emblems.

male name in England at that time was John, but names of saints and French names were also popular choices.[3]

The name *Chaucer* comes from the French word *chaussier*, which means "shoemaker." By the time John Chaucer had named his son Geoffrey at his baptism, however, the Chaucer men had already been well-established wine vintners for several generations. They were solidly middle class. The vintner supplied the owners of taverns with the wine they sold to their customers. He ranked high on the social scale, as wine was the national drink of all classes, with all of it being imported from France. Along with their earned wealth, John Chaucer and his wife owned several homes, which they rented.

There are no specific details about Geoffrey Chaucer's early years, but we do know about the time in which he was born, enabling us to create a profile of a typical child of Chaucer's age and status. Fortunately, stories and documents abound, detailing what it was like to live in Geoffrey Chaucer's time.

Traditionally, children were confirmed in church when they were three, and it is likely that young Geoffrey's confirmation took place at the Church of

St. Martin's-in-the-Vintry. His father had purchased a house in the Vintry ward, or section, of London, where the River Thames came almost to the door. The river was one of the main thoroughfares through the city, and Geoffrey surely witnessed the comings and goings of ships and people from all over the world. London was not as large as Paris, France, or Florence, Italy, but with a population of some 40,000 people, it was the largest city in England. Saint Paul's Cathedral was one of the most impressive buildings to be built in that era, as was the London Bridge, which boasted 20 arches. Swans floated in the water under the London Bridge and children could go swimming on summer evenings, or fish for salmon during the day.

The house that Geoffrey Chaucer called home was similar to others in his neighborhood. The main room, the living room, was called the hall. Chaucer had a sister named Catherine, but little is known about her. The family traditionally slept upstairs, in the bedroom, which was sometimes divided into partitions for privacy. John Chaucer's office was in the house, and there were also several well-paid servants at home.

Geoffrey Chaucer's father worked for King Edward III and his wife, Queen Philippa. The king and queen had a son, also named Edward. He was given the title of Prince of Wales, the same title that Prince Charles of England has today. John Chaucer went abroad with the king and queen to Flanders, where the queen gave birth to her second son, Lionel of Antwerp—who was named after the city where he was born. Fifteen months later, she had another son who was called John of Gaunt—the English pronunciation of Ghent, the city where he was born. The king's and queen's sons would play an important role in Geoffrey Chaucer's life.

When John Chaucer returned to England, he moved his family to Southampton, where he became the deputy to the king's butler. He was responsible for purchasing all of the wine used by the royal family. He also had another important job. He became the collector of customs on woolen goods made in England for export.[4] The Chaucers remained in Southampton for two years and were probably still living there in 1347 when the Black Death, or the plague, hit.

EARLY EDUCATION

By the age of seven, children in medieval London
were viewed as small adults. They were even
dressed in a style similar to that of their parents.
Some historians believe there was not much interest in children during this era, but others have
argued that children were treated quite tenderly.
The average family had five children, and, of
those, usually half survived to adulthood. Young
Geoffrey, like other boys in his class, spent the
first seven years of his life being cared for by
women. Eventually, he began his study at St. Paul's
Cathedral where he was expected to work very
hard and succeed. A high value was placed on
education in Chaucer's time. In fact, there were
more schools in England at the beginning of
the fourteenth century than at the end of the
eighteenth century, 400 years later.[5]

Geoffrey Chaucer would have already learned
his letters at home or perhaps the local parish priest
would have taught him from a small book called a
primer. The first line of the book was called the
"criss cross row" because it began with a large cross,
to remind children of their devotion to God. Most

children knew The Lord's Prayer by the time they entered school. A strict religious education made a deep impression on young Geoffrey Chaucer, as it did on everyone during the Middle Ages. Students were taught that history began with Creation and was scheduled to end in a remote future, with the Second Coming of Christ, followed by the Day of Judgment. The ultimate goal was to achieve glory in the next world, by living a good life in this one.[6] The Black Death had also created a dark cloud of fear in the minds of those who had survived, intensifying the teachings of the church.

At school, Geoffrey was taught in French and Latin, and much of the material was translated from Latin into French. Boys at St. Paul's School studied the Latin classics, which included the writings of Ovid, a Latin poet born in the year 43 B.C. near Rome, Italy. Ovid's most famous work, *Metamorphoses,* was an epic poem that centered on mortal characters, rather than heroes or gods. Ovid's writing appealed to Geoffrey Chaucer. Ovid was a wonderful storyteller who had a sense of fun and an uncritical view of the world, and he wrote about fabulous mythological characters.

Geoffrey Chaucer studied grammar, arithmetic, logic, geometry, and music. People from all classes played music and made it a part of their everyday

Black Death

Bubonic plague, a disease the English called the Black Death, came to England in the cold, wet summer of 1348. Bubonic plague was the most potent illness ever to hit humans. The plague was spread to humans by fleas carried by rats. When the fleas bit humans, the disease was injected into them. Bubonic plague had two forms. One, which was spread by contact, infected the bloodstream, causing the buboes, or inflammation, and internal bleeding. The other, more like pneumonia, spread through respiratory infection. The bubonic plague was nicknamed the Black Death because black spots appeared on the arms, thighs, and other parts of the bodies of infected people. Up until that time, no one was aware of contagious diseases, and there were no vaccinations. Doctors bled their patients, applied hot plaster, and performed other treatments to try to draw poison from the body. Patients were given a variety of ineffective medicines. Physicians were more likely to lives. Bagpipes were one of the most popular instruments among commoners, and, in the upper classes, the fiddle, the harp, and a round, stringed instrument

turn to astrology. They believed that all humans were influenced by the planets.

Many people believed that the plague was the wrath of God. Perhaps the illness had been sent by God to rid the world of the human race. Processions of penance organized by Pope Clement VI only helped to spread the disease. It has been estimated that some 20 million people died across Europe before the plague completely disappeared around 1400, the year Geoffrey Chaucer died. In early outbreaks of the disease, when Chaucer was a young boy, he lost an uncle, a great-uncle, and a cousin in London.

The Black Death would break out six times over the next six decades. In a curious twist, the disease made the Catholic Church richer, as people hoped that, by giving their money to the church, they would receive extra protection. The life of peasants improved over the years because of the disease. The labor force was dying, making the demand for farm workers and servants higher than ever.

Education was highly valued during Geoffrey Chaucer's time. As a boy, he would have studied grammar, arithmetic, logic, geometry, and music.

known as the dulcimer were favored. Astronomy was considered the most noble of the sciences because it connected the study of religion and all things spiritual.

Geoffrey Chaucer's religious education and formal education were balanced by his middle-class life, which exposed him to a wide variety of people.

Because there were few books, and most people could not read, oral storytelling was one of the most popular forms of entertainment for all classes of people. Royalty listened to courtly poetry—lyric verses about love—which had come to them from the French, while the common classes listened to folk verse. Chaucer most likely heard public sermons, which were filled with dramatic storytelling, mystery plays, narrative poems, ballads, and tales. By the time he was ten, he no doubt knew the famous story of *Beowulf,* which had been handed down from Scandinavian invaders hundreds of years before. Perhaps he had listened to the tales of King Arthur and the Knights of the Round Table, and Robin Hood. The Bible was the most popular prose narrative in existence. Children loved games, and there were many to choose from, with football— better known as soccer in the United States—being a favorite. Boys were reminded that they could not play sports inside the cathedral. Hunting was an aristocratic sport, and wrestling was more typical among the common people.

The time of Geoffrey Chaucer's childhood was a transitional period in England. The old feudal

During Geoffrey Chaucer's childhood, the bubonic plague, commonly known as the Black Death, was always lurking in the background.

system was changing because of the Black Death, which had killed so many people. The members of the lower classes started demanding higher wages, because there were fewer people to do all the jobs, and the Black Death continued to lurk in the shadows, waiting to return. In an odd twist of events, the bubonic plague would also play a part in Geoffrey Chaucer's writing career. War had started up again between England and France the year before Chaucer was born, and, in the near future, some citizens would start to rebel against the teachings and the power of the Roman Catholic Church.

Children in the Middle Ages probably did not pay much attention to politics. Like other boys his age, however, when Geoffrey turned 14, he would attain and keep the social status he would have for the rest of his life. Some boys would learn a trade and join a guild that operated much the way unions do today. Others would remain as peasants, tilling the fields. Still others would enter the hallowed world of the Catholic Church. Geoffrey Chaucer would enter the world of the English aristocracy as a page, a young boy being trained for the medieval rank of knight. He would learn how, through his diplomatic nature, to survive the whims and actions of those who ruled his country. Though it would take years, he would also discover his talent for writing, and would be the first to convey the idea that the workings of the heart are universal, regardless of one's social status in life.

Test Your Knowledge

1 What were childbirth and child care like during the 1340s?

   a. Much easier than they are today

   b. No different than they are today

   c. Much more difficult than they are today

   d. Slightly easier than they are today

2 What does the name *Chaucer* mean?

   a. Shoemaker

   b. Seamstress

   c. Butcher

   d. Wine maker

3 For whom did Geoffrey Chaucer's father work?

   a. His wife's family

   b. King Edward III and his wife

   c. The pope

   d. King Henry VIII

4 In what language(s) was Geoffrey Chaucer taught at school?

   a. German

   b. Spanish and French

   c. Latin

   d. French and Latin

5   What was one of the most popular forms of
entertainment for all classes of people?

a. Hunting

b. Playing music

c. Oral storytelling

d. Jousting

ANSWERS: 1. c; 2. a; 3. b; 4. d; 5. c

Chaucer the Young Man

When he was 14 years old, Geoffrey Chaucer became a page in the household of King Edward III's son Lionel of Antwerp and his wife, Elizabeth de Burgh. Geoffrey Chaucer was only five years younger than his employer. Official records indicate that Chaucer wore a short jacket, a pair of red and black hose, and a pair of shoes in his new job as page. The countess bought him several such sets of clothes, and at Christmas she gave him money for necessities.[7]

There was nothing demeaning in medieval times about being a servant. In fact, being of service to the king or his family members raised one's status. Many servants used such positions to establish important contacts in the aristocratic community. A boy started out as a page and graduated to the position of squire, after which he was firmly employed in the royal community. The page was provided free education, and Geoffrey Chaucer's father probably took this into consideration when he placed his son in Lionel of Antwerp's household. He also knew that his son would learn to ride, fight, and hawk, three main activities in a noble's life. A 14-year-old boy in England was considered old enough to begin learning the art of war and was taught combat training. He had to become proficient with a sword and other weapons, and learn the rules about heraldry, or being a messenger. Jousting, a sport in which two mounted knights on horseback tried to unhorse each other using a lance, was another important pastime. It was also common for boys who were older than 14 to carry a dagger, as brawls and street fights were routine.[8]

At the same time, Geoffrey was given the opportunity to continue his studies, especially in the arts and in French and Latin literature. He was introduced to courses such as geometry, law, and elocution, which involved learning how to speak in public. He worked as a scrivener, or correspondent, writing letters for the countess and recording other facts. He was also exposed to fabulous court celebrations, where he would hear poets and other entertainers. Guests would arrive at the castle and stay for weeks. The men would hunt, and at night the tables would be overflowing with food. Entertainment followed the meal. It was during these years that Geoffrey Chaucer first heard the French verse of courtly love.

He learned to play chess and backgammon, sing and dance, play an instrument, and compose. His religious studies continued with the castle's chaplain or a local abbey. In their late teens, men chose between attending Oxford University, Cambridge University, or other colleges to study medicine or prepare for a career in the church.

A more secular, or nonreligious, education was also available at the Inns of Court, and it was there that Geoffrey Chaucer went to study law. Chaucer, ever more interested in poetry, did not complete his law studies, however, which would have taken him 16 years.

BATTLE OF POITIERS

Before Geoffrey Chaucer was born, the English had won a major victory at the Battle of Crecy in France, launching the Hundred Years' War. Another great battle between England and France occurred in 1356, when Chaucer was still a member of Lionel of Antwerp's household. This time, the French sent the biggest army they had ever amassed—some 16,000 soldiers—to fight the invading English. The English were led by King Edward's son, now called the Black Prince because of the color of his armor. The pope stepped in to try to prevent war. He sent two cardinals to meet with both sides to try to arrange a peaceful settlement.

On the day that the Battle of Poitiers was about to begin, one of the cardinals persuaded King Jean, the French king, who was certain of victory, to hold

Before Geoffrey Chaucer was born, the English had
won a major victory at the Battle of Crecy, in France,
launching the Hundred Years' War. Fierce fighting is
depicted between soldiers and knights in armor, above.

off one more day, as it was a Sunday. The cardinal
then went to the English camp and spoke with
Prince Edward, who, certain his troops would not
succeed, was anxious for a settlement before a battle
erupted. He agreed to return the prisoners he had

taken and not to engage in battle or take up arms against the king of France for seven years. King Jean accepted with one condition—the Prince of Wales and 100 of his knights would be taken as prisoners. This, Prince Edward would not agree to, so the French prepared to attack.

The English had the advantage of terrain, and, though they were on the defensive, the soldiers had trained together and fought together through two campaigns. It was a fierce battle, and, in the end, the French lost some 3,000 soldiers, many of them from noble families. King Jean surrendered, and, in 1357, the English took the French king and his young sons back to London as captives. The celebration as they entered London was the greatest ever held. The Prince of Wales rode alongside King Jean, who was dressed in black and riding a tall, white horse.[9] He was staying at the home of John of Gaunt, the king's son, who was now the Duke of Lancaster. King Jean could receive French visitors and continue to live like royalty.

Finally, in 1359, the Treaty of London was signed, but when the French delegates arrived, they refused to agree to the terms that the English had

Beginning of the Hundred Years' War

King Edward III had come to the English throne under violent circumstances. His mother, Isabella, the daughter of King Philip IV of France, and the man she had fallen in love with, Roger Mortimer, had stolen the throne from Isabella's husband, Edward II, through an overthrow of power called a coup d'etat. Edward II had become unpopular with the people, and Isabella knew she could get away with forcibly removing him from power. In 1330, at the age of 15, Edward III assumed power. Among his first acts as king were having Roger Mortimer killed and his mother locked up for the rest of her life. By the time Geoffrey Chaucer was born, around 1340, Edward III was firmly in control of England.

In 1339, the year before Chaucer was born, King Edward III learned that King Philip of France had taken over his French holdings. He became furious and claimed the French throne for himself. After all, his mother had come from French royalty, and he felt entitled. In addition, King Philip's sons had died with no heirs. King Edward was determined to recover the territories that England had once held in France, and the only way he could do that was through military aggression. So began a new era of imperialism, with the goal of the country to attain more power and wealth by invading and conquering other lands.

The English waged a mighty battle against the French at a place called Crecy. With King Philip as their leader, the French were certain of victory. The French knights were great fighters, but England had the advantage because of the creation of a new way of fighting. Welsh knifemen, pikemen, and the trained yeomen who pulled the longbow—in other words, archers—were new additions to the military. When they arrived in France with crossbowmen and English knights forming a great force behind them, the French were confused. The Battle of Crecy was the beginning of a French losing streak to the English, from which it would take almost 100 years for the French to recover.

set. Prince Edward decided to attack France again. He took a large contingent of soldiers and headed to Reims, France, where he intended to be crowned king of France. The French were clever. They had emptied out the countryside, destroying anything that might make life easier for the Black Prince. They did the same in Reims, even burning down the monastery that King Edward had planned to use as his headquarters.

Geoffrey Chaucer was with the English army in Reims as a member of the household of Lionel of Antwerp, now called the Duke of Clarence. While out on a foraging mission, Chaucer was captured by the French and held for ransom. King Edward paid some of the ransom, and his son, the Black Prince, paid the rest.[10] The Black Prince continued on to Burgundy, where he learned that the French had attacked England. Furious, he went on to Paris, but was again puzzled by the lack of aggression from the citizens. It was very difficult to wage war against walled cities and towns.

He was about to launch another attack when a violent storm occurred. Lightning and hailstones killed some 1,000 knights and thousands of horses.

King Edward thought the storm was a sign from God, and changed his mind about trying to claim the French throne. He ransomed the French king for 30 million pounds, which the French agreed to, but actually paid very little of in the end. King Edward was allowed to keep Calais and his land in south-western France independent of the king of France.[11]

Prisoners were exchanged, and King Jean, after living in royal captivity for four years, sailed for France. Geoffrey Chaucer was probably among those sailing back from France with Lionel of Antwerp.

FRANCE AND ENGLAND

Even with such massive conflicts occurring, the French were as comfortable in England as they were in France. King Edward III had spent a great deal of time in France when he was a child. His mother, Isabella, was French. The members of the English aristocracy regularly married Continentals. Chaucer's future wife, Philippa, and her sister Katherine, who later married John of Gaunt, were the daughters of Sir Paon de Roe, a French knight. France was in a central location and was considered by all to be the superpower of the European continent during Chaucer's lifetime. French knights were known for their code of chivalry and for their extraordinary skills in war. France also had an agricultural economy that was working. In terms of combat, architecture, religion, dress, literature, and manners, France set the standards of the day, especially in England.

Things were beginning to change, though, under King Edward's reign. He was gaining so much power from his victories, the French would eventually have to stop thinking of England as one of its many dukedoms, always competing with the others. Not until Joan of Arc emerged in 1429 did France become unified. England, on the other hand, was becoming nationalistic. The English people were beginning to take great pride in their own culture. They felt united as one country, which made them more powerful as a whole.

THE CATHOLIC CHURCH

Meanwhile, religious unrest was growing all over Europe. Discontent was mounting over the expanding power of the Catholic Church, which was spreading its power into the political realm. People all over Europe had grown to dislike the material-ism of the Catholic Church and the worldliness of its representatives. Excessive fees and donations seemed to be cluttering the path to God.

John of Gaunt and Geoffrey Chaucer had become friends, and both were concerned. In 1362, a man named John Wycliff, the king's chaplain, and the first to translate the Bible into English, began speaking out against the Catholic Church. He presented the first hint of the philosophy of Protestantism. Wycliff believed that the pope and the church had too much power over the people. He believed in a faith that was personal and allowed people to interpret the Bible as they saw fit. Further, Wycliff did not believe that during the Rite of Communion the wine and bread became the actual body and blood of Christ. He did not like the idea of the pope having more power than the king. He claimed that all authority derived from God. To emphasize that point, he suggested that priests should not exist as the mediator between humankind and God.[12]

Wycliff had John of Gaunt and Geoffrey Chaucer on his side. The English Catholic bishops were furious over Wycliff's sermons, and they

John of Gaunt and Geoffrey Chaucer were concerned that the pope had more power than the king. They both believed that the pope and the Catholic Church had too much power over the people. John of Gaunt is shown here with the Duke of Lancaster and King John I of Portugal.

wanted to convict him of heresy, a crime punishable by death. At the trial, John of Gaunt broke in with a troop of armed men, preventing Wycliff from being sentenced. After that, everything calmed down for a while. Chaucer, always the keen observer, was also a trained diplomat. He would keep his opinions about the clergy to himself until he began writing *The Canterbury Tales.* He would, however, even then, be known for the way he offered contrasting views of the human experience, rarely inserting his own opinions.

Test Your Knowledge

1 What were three main activities in a noble's life?

a. Jousting, reciting poetry, and hunting

b. Riding, fighting, and hawking

c. Storytelling, riding, and fighting

d. Hawking, playing soccer, and hunting

2 Where did Geoffrey Chaucer study law?

a. Oxford University

b. Cambridge University

c. Inns of Court

d. Harvard University

3 What launched the Hundred Years' War?

a. The Battle of Crecy

b. The Battle of Britain

c. The War of Succession

d. The War of the Roses

4 What happened to Geoffrey Chaucer while he was out on a foraging mission?

a. He got shot.

b. He shot a wild boar.

c. He discovered a secret tunnel.

d. He was captured.

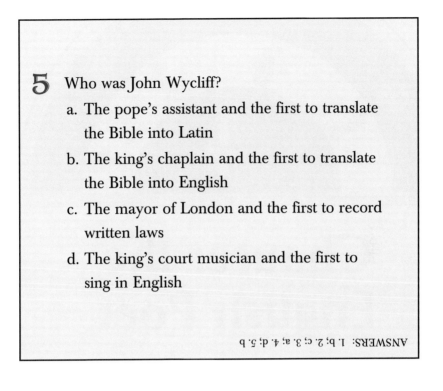

5 Who was John Wycliff?

a. The pope's assistant and the first to translate the Bible into Latin

b. The king's chaplain and the first to translate the Bible into English

c. The mayor of London and the first to record written laws

d. The king's court musician and the first to sing in English

ANSWERS: 1. b; 2. c; 3. a; 4. d; 5. b

Chaucer the English Poet

In 1366, when Geoffrey Chaucer was in his 20s, his father died and his mother remarried a man who had become very wealthy in the wine business. That same year, Geoffrey Chaucer married Philippa Roet, who was from present-day Belgium. Because she was noble-born, she was one of the queen's maidens. Marriage, which fell under the laws of the Catholic Church, was the most important step in the transition to independence. The average marriage age for well-to-do young adults was late teens for young women and early twenties for young men. Usually, an arrangement was made between two families in order for each to know the property values that the spouses owned. The couple was then betrothed, or engaged, and an announcement was made in church on three consecutive Sundays. The wedding itself was celebrated at the door of the church.[13]

The dreaded bubonic plague, the Black Death, returned in France and England in the mid 1360s. It was a disease so lethal that sometimes patients went to bed well and never woke up. There was still no known prevention and no remedy. The second wife of King Jean of France died of the disease. The Duke of Lancaster, probably the wealthiest man in France, also died during this time. His daughter was married to John of Gaunt, who inherited his father-in-law's title and his immense wealth, making him the richest man in the England aside from his father, the king.

During this time, the queen of England became ill and died in London. Hearing that his mother had died, John of Gaunt, who had been fighting in France, returned to England for the funeral. Soon after, he led another fighting expedition across the English Channel. This time, John's wife, Blanche, the Duchess of Lancaster, traveled with him. She would live temporarily in a castle in the country with her ladies as a way of escaping the Black Death, which was taking so many lives in London. Geoffrey Chaucer accompanied the royal couple, and spent much of his time entertaining Blanche with stories and poems.

Despite living in the country, Blanche caught the dreaded disease and died in 1369. Chaucer, who knew her well, sat down to write a commemoration to her, which he titled *The Book of the Duchess*. It was intended as a eulogy, or a farewell, for Blanche, and as a way of consoling her husband, John of Gaunt. The *Duchess* is Chaucer's only writing that is related to a specific event.

CHAUCER THE WRITER

Geoffrey Chaucer began writing in earnest after he married, though he had to write in his spare time. He would recite his poetry, which was the main method of publishing, as there were very few books.

Poetry was much more important in Chaucer's day than it is today, and staged readings were a popular form of entertainment. People gathered in palaces, on the streets, or in country inns to hear poems of romance and adventure being recited. Chaucer had the opportunity when he was young to hear poetry recited in the royal courts and manor homes, and he had paid close attention to the structure of the poems and the way they were delivered.

People in the Middle Ages believed that poetry should deal with human nature and its meaning. The job of the poet was to explain humanity's place in the universe. Love was as important as any of Newton's laws of motion. Love was considered an important way of explaining how the world functioned. It was powerful enough to cause "the crashing of waves against the shore, the flying of sparks toward the sky, and the yearning of Man for God." [14]

A change in literary fashion occurred in the thirteenth and fourteenth centuries. Narratives, such as the *Song of Roland,* or the stories that centered around King Arthur and the Knights of the Round Table, were being replaced with dreams and allegories. An allegory is a story in which the actions of

Poetry was much more important during Geoffrey Chaucer's time than it is today. People gathered in palaces, on the streets, or in country inns to hear poems of romance and adventure being recited. Geoffrey Chaucer is shown here reading his poems to the court of King Richard II of England.

fictional characters serve as symbols that represent moral or spiritual meanings. Medieval audiences liked stories, for example, that served as illustrations of a single human quality, such as tyranny, courage, or fortitude.

Meanwhile, Chaucer remained under the influence of Ovid, who was the first to write about lovesick men. *The Romance of the Rose,* a classic example of courtly poetry written by two Frenchmen, especially influenced Chaucer's writing when he composed *The Book of the Duchess. The Romance of the Rose* was a long thirteenth-century poem. It contained a dream-vision allegory in which a young man fell in love with a rosebud, which symbolized a lady. The second half of the poem, written by Jean de Meun of France, touched on many subjects, including history, religion, sex, love, and women. In it, the old woman told the young man how to succeed in love. However, it was not a poem in favor of women. In fact, the poem made fun of women in a wicked way, creating a shift in the way they were seen by people. Before, women had been written about as angel-like, but this work of satire wrote of nagging, ugly women. It turned the world of courtly

Romance Writing

Romance in the medieval era referred to the word *romanz*, which came from the vernacular French language, or the language spoken by the commoners. All languages derived from Latin were later referred to as Romance languages. Anything written in French was called "romance" to distinguish it from real literature, which was written in Latin.

The term *romance* eventually began to refer to a specific sort of literature, popular among the French-speaking people, about the adventures of knights and their ladies. It dealt with chivalry and courtly love. These adventures were often set in the court of King Arthur, and were particularly popular among the women at court.

The Catholic Church did not approve of these stories because they were not consistent with its strict teachings about marriage. Nonetheless, the stories remained popular with the people. Christian love, with God in charge, was often set against the courtly system of love, with Cupid in charge. Just as people today read romance novels, people in Chaucer's day enjoyed unrealistic tales of male lovers who feared they might never be accepted or proven worthy.

The guidelines for courtly poetry were as follows: When the story opened, someone was usually reading a book, and the reader was introduced to his sleeplessness and dreams. The typical setting was May Day or springtime. The person reading the book had a vision. A guide appeared (often pictured as a helpful animal) and allegorical figures, such as Love, Fortune, and Nature, appeared as characters to help the knight find his way. The classic lover worshiped the woman from afar, trembled in her presence, could not sleep, and had no appetite. The woman of the man's desire was usually older, married, and of a higher social status than the knight. Chaucer followed this formula in *The Book of the Dutchess.*

Courtly love was pure fiction. It was fantasy and was not associated with family or property, the things upon which most marriages were based. It was escapist literature, perhaps for the women who were treated like real estate. Courtly love was supposed to improve a man. He would become more desirable. He would go out of his way to preserve honor for both himself and his lady. Perhaps he would even win more victories in tournaments, inspired by the lady of his desire.

love upside down. Chaucer borrowed heavily from this work when he created the Wife of Bath in *The Canterbury Tales*. He, however, made his woman funny and outspoken.[15]

The Book of the Duchess opened with a man sitting under a tree reading a tragic story by Ovid. He fell asleep and dreamed he was in woods where the emperor was leading a hunt. He came upon a sad knight dressed in black who told the poet that he played a game of chess with Fortune and lost his queen. The knight told of how he fell in love with a beautiful woman and how they lived happily for many years. The dreamer did not understand and asked where she was now. They continued back and forth, with the knight getting more and more frustrated that the dreamer did not understand the woman had died. The exchange between the two became funny, which one did not expect in such a story. Chaucer subtly used the stupidity of the dreamer to force the knight to speak the truth and end his grieving process. A horn sounded, ending the hunt, and the dreamer woke up. Chaucer used this story to tell John of Gaunt to return home with his memories of the lovely Blanche, and move on to his future. The dreamer would turn his dream into a poem.[16]

The fact that this story was steeped in reality set it apart from other works of the time. For the first time, a writer expressed real feelings in a moving poem about a husband's grief. Chaucer had written other poems, but this was a major stylistic departure for him.

WRITING IN ENGLISH

Perhaps even more unique was the fact that Chaucer had decided to write *The Book of the Duchess* in English when everyone else was writing in French. Most of the members of the royal court spoke only French or Latin, though the king knew a little English. The literature of the time, a major part of court life, was written in French. On the other hand, in the mid-fourteenth century, the commoners did not speak French well, if at all. English was their national language.

The tide was changing around language in England. Many of the clerics who had taught French to the children had died during the Black Death, so children in grammar schools started learning their lessons in English. Parliament had always been addressed in French and Latin, but in 1362 the government decreed that all legal proceedings would be carried out in English. That did not actually happen for another 300 years, however.

The common people in England were setting a different standard and creating a new culture. The English were aware after the wars at Crecy and Poitiers—where the English-speaking archers had won over the French knights—that if the victory had been reversed and the French had won, the English language would have disappeared. This made them deeply appreciative of their language.

By the time Geoffrey Chaucer wrote *The Book of the Duchess,* around 1370, English was his chosen language. Most historians agree that Chaucer loved the English language, and he probably thought it was fun to write in the language of the people.[17] To be the first to write consistently in a language required him to find his own style, however. Most poets started by writing in the style they were accustomed to hearing, following the traditions of the times. Chaucer's job was to find a way to combine the courtly style of French poetry with his own English

In the Battle of Poitiers, shown here, English-speaking archers had won over the French knights. The victory made the people of England deeply appreciative of the English language.

verse. Instead of using the standard four-stress line used in *The Romance of the Rose*, Chaucer introduced a five-stress line—iambic pentameter—which was later used by William Shakespeare and John Milton.

THE CONFLICTED WRITER

The same conflicts that existed between the Catholic Church and the people, with regard to the right to think independently, could be said to have existed inside Chaucer. He struggled to write under the accepted guidelines of the day, while his creative self was attempting to emerge. His whole life had been conditioned and controlled, like that of any man in the Middle Ages, by the Roman Catholic Church. When he awoke each morning, he heard church bells. He attended Mass and festivals on holy days, all symbols of the unquestioned authority of the church. He was taught that Earth lay between heaven and hell. Visually, people pictured the universe held in God's arms with humankind at its center.[18] After the Black Death had come and gone twice, people were more controlled by the influence of the clergy, which they hoped could save them.

The problem for Chaucer was that some of these ideas of salvation did not fit with his poetic genius. For poets like Chaucer, Jean de Meun of France, or the great poet Giovanni Boccaccio of Italy, who would become a great influence on Chaucer, it was hard to make deep creativity fit the rigid views of the Catholic Church. When they wanted to write about people as they really were, sometimes making fun of them, the poets would hesitate, asking themselves if what they were doing was a sin. It is obvious from reading Chaucer's works that he loved the world around him. The more realistic his writing became, the more he moved away from the ideal teachings of his religion. The Catholic Church said human passion was evil, and this knowledge was frightening, even to grown men.

Test Your Knowledge

1 When Geoffrey Chaucer's father died, who
   did his mother marry?

   a. A man who had very little money and
      worked as a cloth merchant

   b. A man who worked as an assistant in
      the Catholic Church

   c. A man who had become very wealthy
      in the wine business

   d. A man who was a famous poet and
      musician

2 What caused the death of John of Gaunt's wife?

   a. She died during childbirth.

   b. She died as a result of the Black Death.

   c. She died as a result of the damp, chilly
      air in the castle.

   d. She died as a result of a hunting accident.

3 What was unique about Chaucer's *The Book of
   the Duchess?*

   a. The story was set in the United States.

   b. The story expressed real feelings.

   c. The characters in the story were
      all women.

   d. The story was set in the Middle Ages.

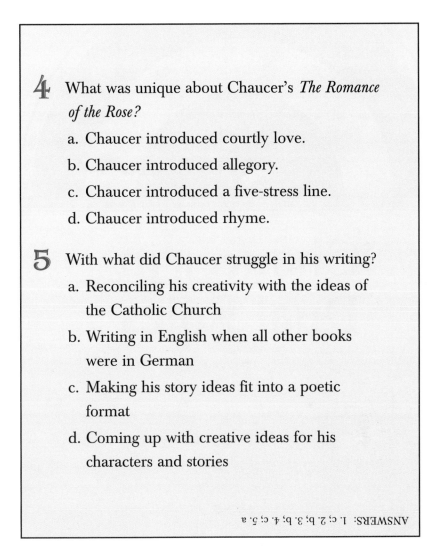

4   What was unique about Chaucer's *The Romance of the Rose?*

   a. Chaucer introduced courtly love.

   b. Chaucer introduced allegory.

   c. Chaucer introduced a five-stress line.

   d. Chaucer introduced rhyme.

5   With what did Chaucer struggle in his writing?

   a. Reconciling his creativity with the ideas of the Catholic Church

   b. Writing in English when all other books were in German

   c. Making his story ideas fit into a poetic format

   d. Coming up with creative ideas for his characters and stories

ANSWERS: 1. c; 2. b; 3. b; 4. c; 5. a

Chaucer in Dual Roles

Geoffrey Chaucer's government career took on added importance when he was in his 30s. Between 1372 and 1373, he went to Italy for the first time. The king had commissioned him to negotiate with the government of Genoa over the choice of an English port for commerce. It was an extraordinary trip for Chaucer. Though it is not known whether or not he met the famous Italian poets Giovanni Boccaccio and Francis Petrarch, he was introduced for the first time to the Italian language and literature, which changed his work.

When he returned to England in 1374, Chaucer was appointed Controller of Customs and Subsidy of Wools, Skins, and Hides in the port of London— an even more important government position. It required him to collect customs, the royal court's main source of income. He also kept the records for the port of London. During that time, he received a prize for apprehending a man named John Kent, who was trying to smuggle a cargo of wool from London without paying the duty on it.

Along with the position came a rent-free house in London. It was actually a mansion at Aldgate, and this would be Chaucer's first time living outside the boundaries of households of royalty. He also received a daily pitcher of wine. John of Gaunt presented Chaucer's wife, Philippa, with expensive cups for three consecutive years, proving the extent of the closeness that existed between the two families. Chaucer was granted wardships in other areas of England during this time. This era of his life was, perhaps, the apex of his government career. He was closely connected to the royal household and he was a successful government employee.

King Edward III, on the other hand, was grieving the death of his oldest son, the Black Prince, who had taken ill while abroad and had become an invalid before he died. The king, depressed and tired, retired to the country, turning the reins of the crown over to his grandson Richard, the only surviving son of the Prince of Wales and Joan of Kent. Richard was ten years old at the time.

In 1376 and 1377, Chaucer made several trips to France to negotiate for peace, and to try to arrange a marriage between Richard and the French king's daughter Marie. The marriage was their only hope for peace, but the young princess died before a marriage could take place. King Edward III died in 1377, so Richard officially inherited the crown. Chaucer went back and forth, trying to arrange a successful marriage for his new king, but his efforts were not successful.

THE ITALIAN INFLUENCE

In 1378, Chaucer was sent abroad again, this time to

Italy on a diplomatic mission. It was time to discuss the ongoing war between France and Italy. The trip enabled him to go to Milan, to the home of one of his favorite writers, Francis Petrarch. Chaucer also knew the works of Dante, who had written *The Divine Comedy*, and he was seeking manuscripts by that great author. Scribes were paid to write out by hand the manuscripts of various writers, so very few copies were ever made. The printing press had not yet been invented. Authors heard of each other through people who had either read their work, or heard it recited.

Chaucer's writing changed after that journey. Historians think of this time as the transition from the French to the Italian phase of his writing. Before, he was writing much like the French writers in his rhythm and tone. After his trip to Milan, Chaucer's writing took on different rhythms.

Chaucer came upon two poems that would have a major effect on his writing style. Both were written by a man named Giovanni Boccaccio, who had been dead for three years when Chaucer arrived in Italy in 1378. Boccaccio's most famous work was *The Decameron*, which means "Ten Days' Work."

Later, Boccaccio's *Testide* became "The Knight's Tale" in Chaucer's *The Canterbury Tales.* Boccaccio also wrote *Il Filostrato*, which bloomed into one of Chaucer's finest works, *Troilus and Criseyde*.[19] It was not uncommon at that time, when very few books were ever published, to borrow from other

King Richard II

Richard II inherited his good looks from his mother, Joan of Kent, considered to be the loveliest woman in England. He wore his golden hair down to his shoulders. He also inherited some darker traits from his parents, which would not serve him well as king. He had his father's uneven disposition. When conditions were favorable, he was quite even tempered and pleasant, but when things did not go his way, he went into a rage. He became obsessed with his murdered great-grandfather, and tried to pattern himself after him. He also inherited his parents' love of luxury and splendor.

The marriage commissioners of England chose an educated and gracious lady, Anne of Bohemia, to be the wife of their king. Richard and Anne were both 15 years old when they married, and loved dances, games, and parties. King Richard was devoted to his writers. Chaucer acquired from Boccaccio something that had much more value than the material in his stories, however—it was the gift of story construction.

Boccaccio's writing had also reflected the times in which he lived, but it seemed to change when the

queen, who was loving and loyal. Richard was the first king to learn English. His interest in architecture and construction was instrumental in the magnificent design of parts of the Westminster Great Hall and the Canterbury Cathedral.

When Queen Anne died suddenly, King Richard had the castle where she had died torn down. His emotional problems reemerged. He thought that nothing could touch him. His spending of the people's money spun out of control. He became suspicious. Sometimes he would go for days without speaking to anyone. He finally became obsessed with his own power. He insisted on being treated as though he were holy, leading to tragic results. William Shakespeare found King Richard's fall from power intriguing enough to write a play called *Richard II.*

Italian poet Giovanni Boccaccio had a great influence on Geoffrey Chaucer's work. In fact, as was common during that time, Chaucer borrowed from Boccaccio's work. Boccaccio's *Testide* became "The Knight's Tale" in Chaucer's *The Canterbury Tales*.

political and cultural climate became more pessimistic. *The Decameron* was a good-natured work, full of humor, but as the tone of the second half of the Middle Ages became more pessimistic, so did the art. Boccaccio wrote a satire on women called *Il Corbaccio* (*The Crow*). He made women appear to be greedy and shallow. He followed this with another work that told of the fall of fortune of great figures of history.

THE HOUSE OF FAME

Chaucer wrote *The House of Fame* sometime between 1374 and 1382. It was divided into three books, with the first being similar in style to *The Book of the Duchess*. Readers were introduced to the authors whom Chaucer had studied, from the historians of Troy to Roman poets like Virgil and Ovid. The lady of *The House of Fame* could give immortality, or enduring fame, to any man she chose. Chaucer was asked by a passerby if he wrote in hopes of becoming famous. Chaucer made it clear that he did not write for that purpose, but to satisfy himself. He also was certain that spending one's life in pursuit of a prize like fame was useless.[20]

The second book really came alive when an eagle came to take the startled dreamer aloft, and began to give a series of lectures. Chaucer, as usual, made fun of himself, portraying himself as a feeble-minded person. The eagle told the poet who wrote of love that he was going to take the poet to a place where he would hear all the tidings of love. The characterization of the eagle was unusual. The narrator was not telling the reader what the eagle represented, but was showing him through his actions and words. This was unique in storytelling. The eagle pointed out various things as they flew to *The House of Fame*, and then the second book ended. Chaucer never finished the third book.

In 1380, Chaucer wrote the poem *The Parliament of Fowls*, which poked fun at the House of Commons. Instead of using the four-stress couplet, Chaucer created the seven-line stanza, which had five stresses to the line. The rhyming pattern was known as Rime Royal.

THE PEASANT REBELLION

Meanwhile, domestic restlessness was growing among the peasants during these years. Like his friend John of Gaunt, Geoffrey Chaucer was conservative when it came to politics. He believed in the old order of things, with the king at the top of the order and the slaves at the very bottom. John of Gaunt, Geoffrey Chaucer, and many others hoped that King Richard would be able to stop the growing influence of the commoners. Unfortunately, King Richard was too young to rule effectively. The French had invaded England soon after the king came into power, and now England was fighting a foreign enemy while facing a growing rebellion at home.

Parliament had done everything in its power to raise money for the war with France, but still more was needed. The Peasants' Revolt occurred in 1381 when the legislators created a poll tax. In order to make the tax work, every citizen had to be counted, so a census was ordered. Citizens began faking their returns. When officials tried to collect the tax by force, the peasants marched on London to obtain charters of freedom for themselves, and to punish the wicked government officials. John of Gaunt became the symbol of their discontent because some of the money was being raised to support him.

The peasants had no legal or political rights. They had no way of changing their status of servitude, unless they rebelled. They wanted their service to the lords to count as rent. Though they were thought of as free citizens, they did not feel free. They had been listening to a group of priests called the Lollards. They wanted a different kind of church. They believed that, because all people were descendants of Adam and Eve, all people should be equal. It was a fanatical movement, born in a time of discontent.

The rebels went first to Canterbury prison and forced the release of a Lollard priest named John Ball, before proceeding on to London, 70 miles away. Along the way, they gained support from craftsmen and small tradesmen, and together they opened prisons and sacked grand manors. They swore to kill as many of the king's servants as they could—including sheriffs, judges, lords, bishops, and dukes—and divide their land among the peasants. They succeeded in killing the Chief Justice of England, Sir John Cavendish, and they wanted John of Gaunt. Twenty thousand of them camped outside London.

The only member of the elite they did not hate was their 14-year-old king, Richard II. He rode

Wat Tyler led a rebel group in London. When Tyler drew his sword against one of the king's squires, the mayor of London turned Tyler's sword against him and killed him. Tyler's death in front of King Richard II is shown here.

among them, wearing a purple robe and a crown, carrying a gold rod, and granting charters to many. Feeling better, many of the peasants returned home believing in their king, but another group entered London, and their leader, Wat Tyler, confronted one of the king's squires. When he drew his sword, the mayor of London killed him with his sword, changing the course of the uprising. John Ball, the Lollard priest, was hanged. All pardons were revoked and the charters were canceled. The Lollards' hope of separating from the Catholic Church was postponed for a very long time.[21]

Chaucer once again did not seem to commit to either side of the dispute with any passion. Years later, however, when he was writing "The Nun's Tale" for *The Canterbury Tales*, his description of the peasants included "terrible yelling of fields in hell."[3]

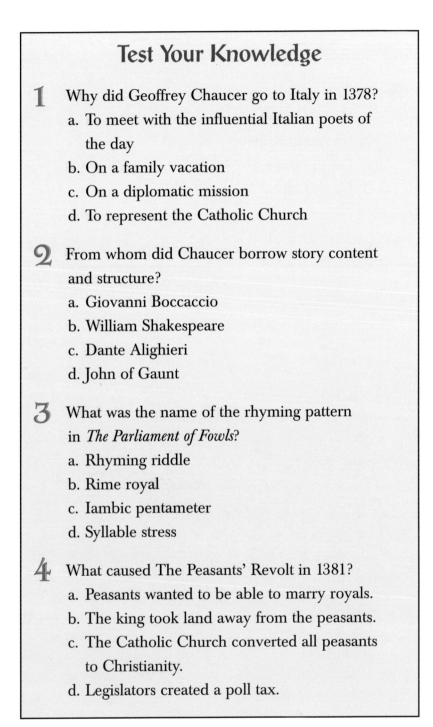

Test Your Knowledge

1 Why did Geoffrey Chaucer go to Italy in 1378?
   a. To meet with the influential Italian poets of
      the day
   b. On a family vacation
   c. On a diplomatic mission
   d. To represent the Catholic Church

2 From whom did Chaucer borrow story content
   and structure?
   a. Giovanni Boccaccio
   b. William Shakespeare
   c. Dante Alighieri
   d. John of Gaunt

3 What was the name of the rhyming pattern
   in *The Parliament of Fowls*?
   a. Rhyming riddle
   b. Rime royal
   c. Iambic pentameter
   d. Syllable stress

4 What caused The Peasants' Revolt in 1381?
   a. Peasants wanted to be able to marry royals.
   b. The king took land away from the peasants.
   c. The Catholic Church converted all peasants
      to Christianity.
   d. Legislators created a poll tax.

5 What happened to John Ball, the Lollard priest?

a. He was hanged.

b. He was knighted.

c. He was sainted.

d. He was shot.

Chaucer in Transition

When Geoffrey Chaucer was about 40 years old, his wife, Philippa, gave birth to their second son, Lewis. Their eldest son, Thomas, was eight, and it is believed that their daughter Elizabeth had become a novice, having been granted probationary membership in the religious community at the Abbey of Barking. In

1381, the year of the Peasants' Rebellion, Chaucer's mother died. He decided to sell his family home, though he would remain at Aldgate. It was turning out to be a transitional year for the poet.

The Peasants' Revolt had been a shock to the country, and, although Chaucer defended human rights, he did not believe in rebellion. He believed that people should accept their positions in society.[22] He was popular with King Richard, who particularly loved his poetry. King Richard was not in favor with everyone, however. He was supposed to be ruling the country with Parliament, but he wanted to raise the level of the monarchy so the king would have all the power.

In 1384, King Richard led some 14,000 soldiers in a battle against Scotland, which turned out to be a big mistake. The Scots retreated and would not be drawn into battle. Parliament had refused to pay off the government's debts, and with these failures occurring, King Richard decided to invade Ireland, which proved to be another big mistake. Members of Parliament, especially the lords who felt that Richard was taking away their power, turned against their king. They fired one of the king's most loyal assistants. King Richard was furious and charged the lords with treason.[23]

Richard's uncle, the Duke of Gloucester, led the opposition. The Earl of Arundel was another noble who opposed the king, and the Earl of Nottingham was the third powerful landowner. John of Gaunt's son Henry Bolingbroke, the Earl of Derby, had also joined the group opposed to the king. Tremendous tension existed among these factions.

It was at this time, in 1384, that Geoffrey Chaucer decided to move to the country. He would share his job as controller with another man. He was also made a royal steward and he probably took his sons with him when he made the rounds to royal estates to inspect the workers. In 1385, he was made justice of the peace, which was not too heavy a burden, as the justices met only four times a year. However, the new position gave him the opportunity to observe up close criminals of every variety. Some formed the basis for characters in his later writing.

THE LEGEND OF GOOD WOMEN

Chaucer was constantly writing poems and stories during these days. In 1386, he wrote *The Legend of*

Good Women, which was dedicated to Anne of Bohemia, King Richard's wife. The story, French in tone, was charming in its attitudes toward women. For unknown reasons, however, it was never finished. It is filled with "inside" jokes that were popular in the royal court at the time. The woman in Chaucer's *The House of Fame* had been unfaithful to her husband, but this time Chaucer made a point of creating very faithful women. They were so faithful to their husbands that, even when their husbands strayed from their wives, the women remained faithful. In *The Legend of Good Women,* Chaucer painted men as wicked, unreliable, and unfaithful. The only man who was really trustworthy was none other than the character of Geoffrey. Men, he declared, should be compassionate and merciful, and loyal to those who serve them.[24] Perhaps Chaucer was thinking of the men who were opposing his king.

TROUBLE AT HOME

Meanwhile, in 1386, France was again making plans to go to war with England when Chaucer decided to enter politics. Geoffrey Chaucer, always loyal to his king, had agreed to serve in the House of Commons as a representative from Kent. Parliament at that time was "a political experiment of sorts," and was not taken very seriously.

Meanwhile, tensions were mounting among the lords who did not like what the king was doing. A man named De Vere, a strong supporter of the king's, along with other supporters, went to battle against the lords. De Vere was defeated and the lords went to London to remove the king from the throne. They also had four of his favorite knights killed. The lords ruled for a short time, but not well. Two of them, including King Richard's cousin, changed their loyalty back to the king. At age 22, Richard was reinstated as king.[25] Throughout it all, Chaucer had tried to keep a low profile.

Chaucer took on a new title, Chief Clerk of the King's Works, a job that put him in charge of construction projects, such as the Tower of London and Westminister Abbey. His wife, Philippa, died in 1387, which must have been a terrible shock.

A WRITING MASTERPIECE

Chaucer had started writing *Troilus and Criseyde* in the 1380s, when he was at the height of his craft.

Women in the Middle Ages

The Romance of the Rose, one of the most popular stories in medieval England, was filled with malicious satire about women. The story was a reaction to the way women had been idealized in courtly poetry. In the *fabliaux*, women were painted as over-talkative, unsettled, wanton, and quarrelsome. This kind of writing, along with the teachings of the Catholic Church, depicted women as monsters. In the Middle Ages, anger was largely associated with women.

Sir Thomas Aquinas thought that women, who were judged as inferior to men, needed to be governed by those wiser than themselves. They were taught at a young age to be obedient to their fathers, and later to their husbands. The Catholic Church considered a woman to be a temptress and an obstacle to holiness. Another general belief supported by the church said that, in the Bible, Eve caused Adam to lose Paradise, and women forever after would have to pay for that. From the book of Genesis and the story of the fall of mankind through the sin of sex, man would forever be burdened with guilt, a guilt that only Christ could redeem. It seemed that, as men neared the end of their lives, and worried about going to hell, their perception of women as nasty and evil grew stronger.

Women were also severely criticized for their focus on fashion, and for their vanity. They were said to be too occupied with children and housekeeping to have the time to think about divine things.

Women were criticized for gossip and chatter, for craving sympathy, for being coquettish, sentimental, over-imaginative, and over-responsive to students and other beggers. They were scolded for bustling in church, saying prayers aloud, kneeling at every shrine, paying attention to anything but the sermon.*

One cannot blame women of the era who did behave like shrews. They were, no doubt, angry over the many harsh judgments bestowed upon them by men.

* Barbara W. Tuchman, *A Distant Mirror: The Calamitous 14th Century*. New York: Ballantine Books, 1978, p. 356.

King Richard II, in happy times, presides over a tournament. In 1386, however, tensions were mounting among the lords who did not like what the king was doing.

Astrology was considered an important science during the Middle Ages, and Chaucer was knowledgeable in it. *Troilus and Criseyde* was based on the rare astrological phenomenon of Jupiter and Saturn in the sign of Cancer.

Troilus and Criseyde was written as if Chaucer had wanted to bring together all the great authors he had read and loved in this work. He took two minor characters from Homer's *Iliad*—Troilus and Criseyde—and created his own work. He also borrowed some major characters from Homer's *Iliad*—Priam, Hector, and Achilles, to name a few. Adapted from Boccaccio's *Filostrato*, Chaucer made the setting more vivid and gave the dialogue humor and a more natural feel.

Chaucer's tale was a love story. Troilus, the son of the Trojan king, Priam, fell in love with Criseyde during the Trojan War. When he saw Criseyde, he sighed, grew pale, and could not eat. He felt timid and afraid of rejection, so he relied on his uncle to make the relationship work. When he was rejected, it was as if the world had stopped spinning on its axis. It was common for medieval characters to indulge in bouts of self-pity, and threaten to kill themselves when feeling abandoned. It was also common for people in medieval England to express their feelings more openly than they do today.

Criseyde's father had joined the Greeks and was considered a traitor. The two lovers, however, with some help, managed to spend three years together in perfect harmony in Troy. When prisoners were exchanged, Criseyde was forced to go to her father's side, but she swore to love Troilus forever. She further swore to return within ten days, but on the way to her see her father, she fell in love with her Greek escort, Diomede, and gave him the pin Troilus had given her. The devastated Troilus was killed in battle by Achilles, and Criseyde was set up as the unfaithful woman.[26]

Chaucer focused on the psychological aspects and motive and mental states of his characters. The notion of fate was one of the strongest elements of the poem, and the conventions of courtly love were once again essential to an understanding of the poem. Love was considered a fine art, and the pursuit of love was intended to ennoble the character. Love was a topic that would occupy Chaucer until his death.

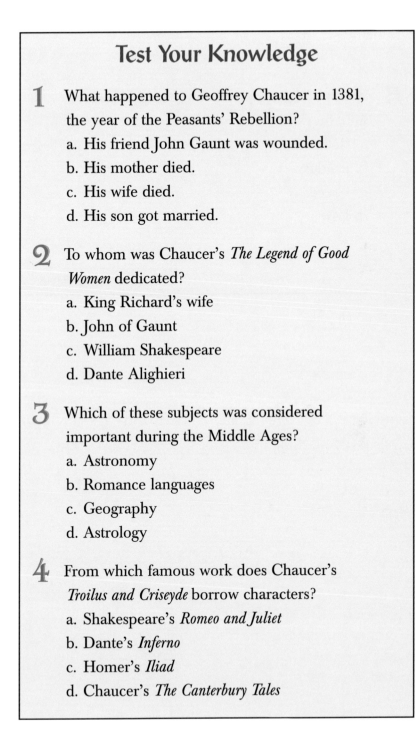

Test Your Knowledge

1   What happened to Geoffrey Chaucer in 1381, the year of the Peasants' Rebellion?

   a. His friend John Gaunt was wounded.

   b. His mother died.

   c. His wife died.

   d. His son got married.

2   To whom was Chaucer's *The Legend of Good Women* dedicated?

   a. King Richard's wife

   b. John of Gaunt

   c. William Shakespeare

   d. Dante Alighieri

3   Which of these subjects was considered important during the Middle Ages?

   a. Astronomy

   b. Romance languages

   c. Geography

   d. Astrology

4   From which famous work does Chaucer's *Troilus and Criseyde* borrow characters?

   a. Shakespeare's *Romeo and Juliet*

   b. Dante's *Inferno*

   c. Homer's *Iliad*

   d. Chaucer's *The Canterbury Tales*

5 Which of these topics would occupy Chaucer until his death?

a. Religion
b. Jealousy
c. Greed
d. Love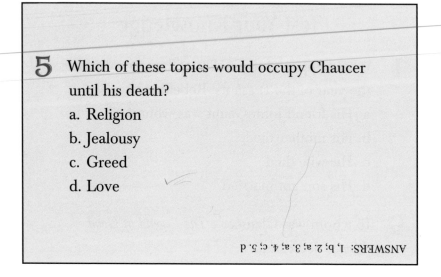

ANSWERS: 1, b; 2, a; 3, a; 4, c; 5, d

Chaucer and
The Canterbury Tales

I n 1387, when he began writing *The Canterbury Tales*, Geoffrey Chaucer was more detached from the royal court—both physically and emotionally—than he had ever been. He was living in the town of Greenwich, and, from his house, he could watch pilgrims making their way to Canterbury. Perhaps he even went on such a pilgrimage.

English politics, with King Richard II at the helm, had settled down a bit.

Chaucer must have known that his "tales," told by people of the middle class, would not have much appeal to those in the royal court, who would have found the content inappropriate. His audience would be a cross-section of English society at the time, mainly the middle class, which included neither extreme on the social scale. The tales were written with the male reader in mind. This period in Chaucer's writing would become known as his English period. Not only did Chaucer write in English, but he also presented characters whose English nature was self-evident.

The characters in *The Canterbury Tales* were on a 60-mile, four-day trip to Canterbury Cathedral, to the shrine of Thomas Becket. England was full of shrines, but perhaps the most popular was this shrine of the murdered archbishop of Canterbury. Monks were available to guide the bands of pilgrims, to show them the banner and painted glass, and the holy shrine in the Trinity Chapel, which had more jeweled wealth than anything else in England.

A wonderful drama unfolded when the host, Harry Bailey, told the travelers that they were to compete by telling stories. The prize was a supper at the Tabard Inn, to be paid for by all of the other travelers. The general prologue, the beginning of the book, introduced all of the pilgrims except the Canon and the Yeoman. The prologue functioned as the first act. No one can be sure of the order in which Chaucer organized the stories of his characters, but most scholars follow the order of the Ellesmere manuscript, dating back to approximately ten years after Chaucer's death in 1400.[27] The characters and their tales were arranged as follows: Knight, Miller, Reeve (Estate Manager), Cook, Man of Law, Wife of Bath, Friar, Summoner; Clerk, Merchant; Squire, Franklin (landowner), Physician, Pardoner; Shipman, Prioress, Sir Thopas, Melbee, Monk, Nun's Priest; Second Nun, Canon's Yeoman; Manciple (Business Manager), and Parson. The details in the prologue were repeated in the stories, so that when various pilgrims began to tell their tales, the reader was quite aware of specific traits of each character, such as the Wife of Bath's deafness.

Thomas Becket

Approximately 150 years before Geoffrey Chaucer was born, a murder occurred in the Canterbury Cathedral in England. The crime left such an impact on the people that the murdered man was deemed a martyr. The murdered man was Thomas Becket, Archbishop of Canterbury.

There was a constant power struggle in the twelfth century between the king and the pope, with both trying to exercise the most influence on the people. Becket was introduced to King Henry I in 1154, soon after he had been made Archbishop of Canterbury, and they became friends. After the Archbishop of Canterbury died in 1161, King Henry seized the opportunity to increase his influence over the Catholic Church. He told the pope that he wanted to name Becket to the highest position in the Catholic Church in England. The pope agreed.

Becket shifted his allegiance from the king to the church, in a move that felt like a serious betrayal to King Henry. When the king accused Becket of theft, Becket fled to France and remained there in exile for six years. During this time, he excommunicated the bishops of London and Salisbury for supporting the king. They were banished from the church. In 1170, however, the two former friends met in Normandy and seemed to resolve their argument. Becket returned to Canterbury as archbishop, but he refused to forgive the bishops. King Henry was outraged again.

Four of the king's knights were inspired to sail to England to kill Becket. A monk named Edward Grim saw everything from his hiding place. He wrote that the knights entered the cathedral and demanded that Becket restore the bishops to communion. Becket refused. According to the monk's account, Becket declared that he was ready to die, if he had to. When the knights tried to remove him from the church, he clung to a pillar. He was beaten until he died.

King Henry was unnerved, and sent the knights away in disgrace. Several miracles were rumored to have occurred at the Canterbury Cathedral, and Thomas Becket was soon canonized. A shrine was created at the cathedral. Four years after Becket's death, the king put on a sack cloth and walked barefoot through the streets of Canterbury in an act of penance. Monks flogged King Henry with branches, and the king spent the night in Becket's crypt.

The travelers rose to the occasion, and as each one stepped forward, it was as if a miracle had occurred for the reader. For the first time in history, the characters in a work of fiction were not coming from a dream vision, or behaving in expected ways. Through Chaucer's imagination, and through his brilliance at creating characters that "lived" on the pages, he changed the face of literature.

Chaucer started the tales with a knight who was honorable and courteous to all, courageous in war, and who understood the religious significance of a pilgrimage. His son the Squire was a courtly lover who knew how to sing, dance, and joust. He was dressed in the latest fashion. His hair was "curled as if taken from a press" and he "blazed like a spring meadow to the sight."[28]

Next, readers met the Prioress, Madame Eglantine, who spoke French with a perfect accent and was a perfect lady. Chaucer obviously loved this character, who had several little dogs. She was tender-hearted and had a small red mouth, a straight nose, blue eyes, and the high forehead that all the ladies desired to have. In her innocent heart, the church and the world existed comfortably side by side. The Miller had his bagpipes; the Monk had his hunting dogs; and the Wife of Bath wore a shady hat.[29] It was this kind of attention to detail that made each individual character stand out.

Chaucer presented himself in most of his writings as "bookish, fat, nearsighted, comically pretentious, slightly self-righteous, and apparently—because of a fundamental lack of sensitivity and refinement—thoroughly unsuccessful in the chief art of medieval heroes: love."[30] A portrait of him in the Ellesmere copy of *The Canterbury Tales* revealed a man with gray, short hair. He was heavyset, with a large nose and dark, hooded eyes.

It was the pilgrimage that linked the stories of the travelers together. The pilgrimage that Chaucer designed in his writing showed the reader how the people of England in the late medieval era really were, and the tales showed us how they thought they were.[31]

Chaucer's pilgrims behaved the way real people do. They were not patient, and they jumped in, interrupting each other to tell their own tales. This kind of interaction reflected England at that time. It was a country where people were questioning the

The pilgrimage to the Canterbury Cathedral is the common element that links all of the travelers' stories together. This stained glass window from the Canterbury Cathedral depicts the pilgrims on their way to the cathedral.

beliefs and moral character of the Catholic Church, where the old system of feudalism was falling apart, and where there was a stronger middle class with land and rank being replaced by money. Chaucer was trying to make sense of this world. Maybe he wanted to create a world where a variety of people had to work toward a simple, common goal—of getting somewhere.

There were more serious tales than humorous ones, but Chaucer maintained a fine balance, creating humor when things get too bogged down in serious-ness. Themes included the nature of love, what made a good ruler, what defined a good life, and what caused innocent people to suffer. *The Canterbury Tales* included all the known literary genres of the time. Chaucer used the familiar romance style to tell the tales of the Knight, the Squire, the Clerk, and the Wife of Bath. The tales of the Miller, the Reeve, the Shipman, the Summoner, the Cook, and the Merchant incorporated various forms of French *fabliaux*, funny and often obscene stories, which we would refer to today as dirty stories.

"The Nun's Priest's Tale" was an example of a beast fable, in which animals behaved like human beings. The Man of Law and the Physician characters told classical legends. Moral allegories known as *exemla*, a sermon, and literary confession were also used.

It would be impossible to give an in-depth analy-sis of *The Canterbury Tales* in a few pages, but it is worth touching on one subject that absorbed the pilgrims—marriage, or the relationship between men and women. The main question dealt with whether the man or the woman was "the boss" in a marriage. The cluster of stories in *The Canterbury Tales*

In *The Canterbury Tales*, the stories of the Miller, the
Reeve, the Shipman, the Summoner, the Cook, and
the Merchant incorporated various forms of French
fabliaux, funny and often obscene stories, which we
would refer to today as dirty stories.

that refer to this theme are sometimes called the
"marriage group," though almost all of the nonreligious stories deal with some aspect of love.

The character of the Physician, shown here, told a classical legend.

With so many stories devoted to love and marriage, one cannot help but wonder whether Chaucer was happy in his own marriage. From his writing, one assumes so. He suggests in *The Book of the Dutchess* that a woman's love brings salvation, and the happiness of marriage is compared to the happiness of heaven in his poetry. Instead of presenting idealized versions of love, Chaucer put an emphasis on the ordinary, commonplace love of a husband for a wife.

This theme is still popular today. When psychologist David Buss, author of *The Evolution of Desire*, was asked in a recent article in *The New York Times*, "What do you believe is true even though you cannot prove it?" he replied, "True love." He added that "while love is common, true love is rare, and I believe that few people are fortunate enough to experience it."[32] Chaucer just might have agreed.

Test Your Knowledge

1 What was the period in which Chaucer wrote
The Canterbury Tales known as?

a. His tragic period

b. His humorous period

c. His English period

d. His romantic period

2 What did *Canterbury Tales* host Harry
Bailey tell the travelers they were
competing for?

a. A free night's stay at the Tabard Inn

b. A trip to Chaucer's hometown

c. A pilgrimage to Canterbury Cathedral

d. Supper at the Tabard Inn

3 What linked together the stories of the
travelers in *The Canterbury Tales*?

a. The pilgrimage

b. A shared love of poetry

c. A desire for romance

d. Their love of food

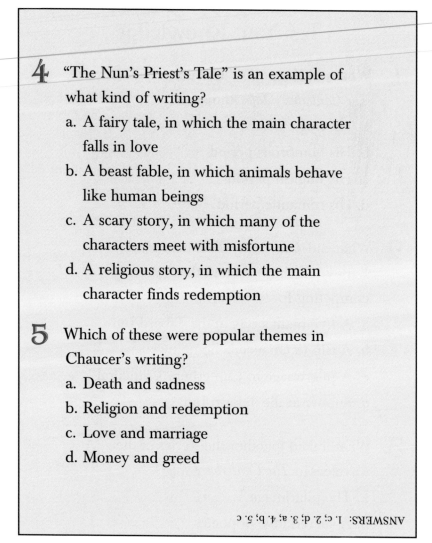

4 "The Nun's Priest's Tale" is an example of
what kind of writing?
  a. A fairy tale, in which the main character
     falls in love
  b. A beast fable, in which animals behave
     like human beings
  c. A scary story, in which many of the
     characters meet with misfortune
  d. A religious story, in which the main
     character finds redemption

5 Which of these were popular themes in
Chaucer's writing?
  a. Death and sadness
  b. Religion and redemption
  c. Love and marriage
  d. Money and greed

ANSWERS: 1. c; 2. d; 3. a; 4. b; 5. c

Chaucer and the Theme of Marriage

Marriages among the elite went far beyond love and compatibility between two people. They were, in fact, a major opportunity to acquire territory, power, and political alliances. When royal families were looking for mates for their children, the brides' and grooms' feelings about the union were not considered.

An heiress could be sold as though she were real estate. Love was not the goal in upper-middle-class marriages. In fact, love between a husband and wife was viewed as almost impossible.

Conditions were better for a middle-class woman. Women of their status were almost as independent as men, and they had many more rights than women in the Victorian era would have centuries later. In the business world, the middle-class woman was as free as a man. She could run her own business, join a guild, and even argue a court case for herself.

It could be said that a woman was better off being single. Once married, the woman always came second to her husband. If her husband died or was killed, however, a widow had a tremendous amount of freedom. She even gained ownership of the property her husband had left behind. She married again only if she wanted to. A woman born into the feudal system was the unluckiest, for she either had to marry or join a convent. Even peasant women, however, could hold tenancies and collect rent. In the guilds, women had control of certain trades, usually spinning and ale-making.[33]

THE CHURCH AND MARRIAGE

Church courts set the guidelines for marriage, and they were rarely challenged, as the church was considered to be all-knowing. When a woman was betrothed to a man through her parents, the bride's parents would often give a portion of their land to the man. The bride was expected to serve her husband in times of peace and war—and in the drudgery of daily domestic chores. Girls were taught how to be good wives, how to please their husbands, and how to nurture their children.

It was not considered a crime for a man to beat his wife. In fact, lords of chivalry were known to beat their wives. The custom was practiced without shame. The only way the woman was able to defend herself was with her words. Words could give her mastery in the household, but she ran the risk of being beaten if her words did not sit well. If a daughter refused to marry the man her parents had selected for her, she was beaten and locked up, and no one would come to her defense.[34]

The rulebooks for marriage and relationships were written by men. Women were told they should not be arrogant, answer back, or contradict their husbands, especially in public. Women were only to obey.

THE MARRIAGE GROUP

The "Tale of Melibeus" and the "Nun's Priest's Tale" in *The Canterbury Tales* asked whether a husband could accept his wife's advice. The first of these tales claimed that accepting his wife's advice was a wise thing for a man to do, while the second showed how disastrous it was for a man to take such advice.

All of the discussion on marriage brings us back to the character of the Wife of Bath, which became a different version of Chaucer's *The Romance of the Rose*. The Wife of Bath was based on a favorite joke of the Middle Ages, the domineering wife. Dame Alice did not hesitate to admit that she had faults. She was a scold, and she was coarse, dishonest, and sensual, which, in the way Chaucer presented her, was part of her charm. Her role in *The Canterbury Tales* was an important one because her creator allowed her to speak her mind about marriage.

The Clerk of Oxford, a student, stepped forward next. He was the opposite of Alice. He, like a priest, was a man focused on moral virtue. Dame Alice

The character of the Wife of Bath was based on a favorite joke of the Middle Ages, the domineering wife. In *The Canterbury Tales*, Chaucer allows this character to speak her mind about marriage.

stood for everything that he despised. He has not forgotten that, at one point, Dame Alice said that no clerk could speak well of women. This provoked the Clerk to tell the story of Griselda, the most patient wife who ever lived.

Griselda, more than any other woman in literature at the time, appealed to male authors. In the fourteenth century, Boccaccio created her character in *The Decameron.* The Clerk of Oxford in *The Canterbury Tales* used allegory, making Griselda the personification of patience. Petrarch wrote the same story in Latin, while a French writer named Menatier also wrote about the patient Griselda as the kind of woman every man wanted.

The Clerk repeated back, in a calm tone, everything that the Wife of Bath had said, but coming from his mouth, she seemed like a ranting, raving fool. Griselda, the Clerk explained, did all that her husband told her to, even allowing each of her children to be taken away to be killed. At the end of his story, the Clerk made the point that, if a woman could patiently survive whatever a man did to her, we all should consider accepting whatever God sends our way. Chaucer, it is believed, was a bit ashamed of the story and, in reality, advised noble wives not to obey men who mistreated them.

The Merchant, newly married, offered a bitter story of an old noble knight who married a maiden, who, in turn, was loved by a squire. The squire, of

The character of the Merchant, newly married, offered a bitter story of an old noble knight who married a maiden, who, in turn, was loved by a squire. A knightly scene with a herald and a lady is shown in this fourteenth-century painting.

course, finally won the young maiden. All three characters were portrayed as fools. Chaucer used satire in this story to point out the foolishness of marriage as an excuse for lust. Next, Chaucer brought in the Squire, who told a tale of the ideal romance. That tale was never finished, however.

Chaucer had included so far a wife who dominated her husband, a husband who dominated his wife, a young wife who fooled her old husband, and a pure wife who fussed and stirred up trouble. It was the Franklin, however, who spoke about true love, with neither spouse competing for mastery. His tale was also about a knight, and included a lady and a lovesick squire. However, this knight and his lady loved each other as friends and equals. When her knight went to war, a squire approached the lady. She told him that he could have his way with her if all the rocks on the Brittany Coast were cleared away—a task that she knew was impossible to achieve. When the squire paid a magician to remove the rocks, the lady told her husband. Though his heart was breaking, he told her she must keep her promise. The squire did not hold her to her promise, but he had to return to the magician and tell him that he could not pay him the full price he had offered him. The magician asked him if he has succeeded with the lady, and the squire told him the truth. The magician, pleased with everyone's behavior, told the squire he did not even want the money. The Franklin's message about marriage was that love creates success. The best way to be free is to give freedom, and whoever loved someone should allow them to be free. When, in his later years, Chaucer wrote "The Franklin's Tale," the idea that marriage could be based on love was radical.

Characters and Events from Life

Operating under the assumption that all fiction is at least somewhat autobiographical, it is tempting to try to match various characters in fictional stories to real people in the author's life. We know that writers of Chaucer's time borrowed from other writers. It is an intriguing exercise, then, to see which characters and events from real life Chaucer put into *The Canterbury Tales*. Below are a few examples.

The host, Harry Baily, had a name similar to that of Henricus Bailly or Baillif, an innkeeper in Southwark. He was also a member of Parliament from that borough. The character of the Shipman was believed to be based on a sailor named Peter Risshenden, who sailed a ship called the *Maudelayne*. Some experts speculate, however, that this character was based on a man named John Piers.

Dame Alice, The Wife of Bath, was assumed to be Alice Perrers, the mistress of King Edward III. The knight was thought to be a portrait of

Enguerrand VII, or Enguerrand de Coucy, the son of
Enguerrand VI and Catherine of Austria, who were
in an aranged marriage, mastered by the king of
France and the Duke of Austria. The knight, among
all the characters, was the noblest of the pilgrims. He
matched the real-life profile of a man named Thomas
Pynchbek. The Canon was supposedly modeled after
William Shuchirch, of the king's chapel at Windsor,
who dabbled in alchemy (as many intellectuals did).

"The Monk's Tale" expressed Chaucer's scorn
for disrespectful and unruly commoners. In *The
Canterbury Tales*, Chaucer described the Friar as
corrupt and hypocritical. The clergy on the whole
were supposed to be closer to God, but often the
contrary was true. Priests were underpaid, so they
were quick to sell their services. Offerings were
expected for every service they performed, even for
Communion. They also took bribes.

The Pardoner was painted as the most evil of
the pilgrims because he used the church and sacred
objects for personal profit. In 1378 and 1379, two
men battled over which one of them would be the
next pope. The bishops of England tried to force
people to accept Pope Urban, who raised money by
offering to forgive the sins of a soul, dead or alive,
for money. When Chaucer wrote the "Tale of the
Pardoner," he made fun of the notion of selling pardons.

The so-called "marriage group" of Chaucer's tales began and ended with a debate. The solution that the Franklin offered was no doubt that which Geoffrey Chaucer believed.

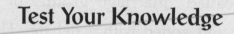

Test Your Knowledge

1　Aside from love and compatibility, what were marriages among the elite about?
   a. Acquiring territory
   b. Acquiring power
   c. Forming political alliances
   d. All of the above

2　Who set the guidelines for marriage in Chaucer's time?
   a. Priests
   b. Local officials
   c. Church courts
   d. Legal courts

3　What literary tool did the Clerk of Oxford in *The Canterbury Tales* use?
   a. Courtly love
   b. Allegory
   c. Iambic pentameter
   d. Rhyming verse

4　What was the Franklin's message about marriage?
   a. Love creates success.
   b. Love creates heartache.
   c. Success brings love.
   d. Success brings heartache.

5   On which radical idea was "The Franklin's Tale" based?

a. Marriage could be based on social status.

b. Marriage could be based on greed.

c. Marriage could be based on love.

d. Marriage could be based on wealth.

ANSWERS: 1. c; 2. b; 3. b; 4. a; 5. c

Chaucer's Final Years

Chaucer was mugged twice on English roads, before he finally was given a less demanding job as a steward of the royal forest at Petherton in 1391. He had already begun work on *The Canterbury Tales*, and was probably grateful to be released from so much responsibility.

Political unrest in England was growing again, and, in 1395, something happened that triggered rebellion. The Lollards put a list of things they did not like on the door of St. Paul's Cathedral. Among the Lollards were two of Chaucer's friends, Sir Lewis Clifford and Sir Richard Stury. They did not believe in war, capital punishment, pilgrimages, and the Catholic Church's ruling that clergy could not marry. The church came down hard on them, and Sir Lewis was made to recant, or admit to being a traitor to God. The teachings of the church caused people to die in terror of what awaited them. When Queen Anne died in 1394, she had repented for having been too fond of parties. Later, Chaucer would also be affected by the power of the Catholic Church.

King Richard, after the death of his queen, married Isabella, an eight-year-old French princess. He also became unpredictable. Chaucer wrote a piece at this time called *Lak of Stedfastnesse*, addressed to the king.

O prince, desyre to be honourable,
Cherish thy folk and hate extorcioun.
Suffre nothing that may be reprevable
To thyn estat don in thy regioun.

Shew forth thy swerd of castigacioun,
Dred God, do law, love trouthe and worthinesse,
And wed thy folk agein to stedfastnesse.[35]

King Richard did not listen to Chaucer's advice. In 1397, he sought revenge against the men who had caused him humiliation eight years earlier. He accused the Duke of Gloucester and the Earl of Arundel of treason, and had them killed. In March 1399, immediately after John of Gaunt died, King Richard seized the property that John had left to his son Henry of Bolingbroke. King Richard had forgotten that Henry was very popular with the people, and when Henry returned to England for his inheritance, no one wanted to oppose him. Henry had Richard deposed, which meant he had to give up his crown. He was put in prison. Henry, with the approval of the people, made himself the constitutional monarch of England. He was now King Henry IV. Little Isabella was sent back to France to her father.

King Henry IV and Geoffrey Chaucer had known each other for all of Henry's life. The king gave Chaucer money and gifts. In 1398, Chaucer moved into a house next to Westminister Abbey. He

King Richard led a failed attempt to gain revenge against the men who had humiliated him eight years earlier. The Parliament at Westminster is shown here deposing King Richard II and proclaiming Henry IV as king.

complained, however, that because of age he could not write the way he used to. Meanwhile, he continued working on *The Canterbury Tales.* Chaucer did not follow the custom of the day by creating a manuscript to give to his patron, perhaps because he finished very few of his works.

King Richard died at the end of February 1400, and Chaucer died on October 25, 1400, probably from the Black Death. At the very end of his life, he was overwhelmed by the sins he had committed. He had written about the love between men and women, a sin for which he repented. The conflicts that he had suffered while writing had never gone away. He was buried in the Poet's Corner of Westminster Abbey.

Between 1398 and 1403, Chaucer's son Thomas had settled in a town approximately ten miles from Oxford. He married a wealthy heiress, Maud Bergersh, in 1395 and from this marriage he acquired a beautiful manor estate and other valuable properties. Over the years, he became even more successful in the commercial world than his father had been. In 1399, he was appointed as the constable of Wallingford Castle. Then, in 1400, the year of his father's death, he was made sheriff of Oxfordshire, and in 1402 he became the king's butler. Eventually, he became a member of Parliament for Oxforshire and served in 13 other parliaments.

The literary elite gathered at Thomas Chaucer's home regularly. A good friend of his, John Lydgate, became a well-known poet and wrote a ballad to Thomas Chaucer. It was among these people that English as the national language developed. Some believed it started when a group of friends who had

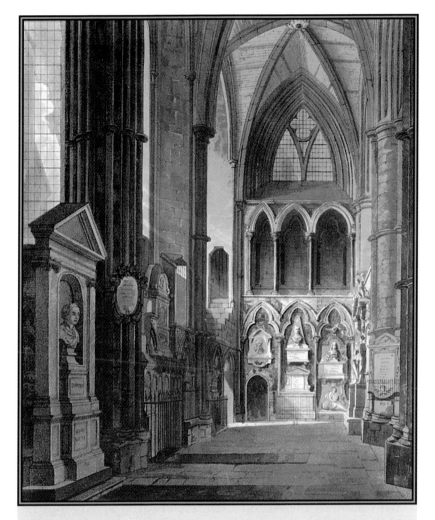

When Geoffrey Chaucer died in October 1400, he was buried in the Poet's Corner of Westminster Abbey. The entrance into Poet's Corner is shown here.

attended Oxford together, including Thomas Chaucer, decided to organize and publish Geoffrey Chaucer's poetry.

A New Century

C haucer died in 1400, the same year that King
Richard II died, at the turn of the century.
Before King Richard died, Henry IV of England
had to stop a rebellion started by the earls of Kent,
Huntington, and Salisbury. They wanted Richard
restored as king of England. Henry IV had them
killed because of this loyalty to their king. Henry IV
died in 1413 and was succeeded by his son Henry V.
A new era of firearms began, and Henry V repeatedly
attacked France

In 1429, Jeanne d'Arc, or Joan of Arc, led the
French against the English and won. This turned the
tide of the Hundred Years' War. By the middle of the
century, there was more stability in Europe, thanks
to the efforts of successful leaders, such as England's
King Henry VII. The Renaissance that started in Italy
in the fourteenth century came into full bloom mid-
century, producing such artists as Leonardo da Vinci,
who painted the *Mona Lisa*. Celebrated artists and
poets produced some of the greatest works of the
time. Christopher Columbus was born in Spain in
1451, and he would play a large role in changing
people's perceptions about the shape of the world.
The Dark Ages, a term made up by Geoffrey
Chaucer's former mentor, Francis Petrarch, to
describe the 900-year period that started in 410
and went to the time of the Renaissance, were over.

Geoffrey Chaucer's works were not printed for a large audience until some 100 years after his death. *The Canterbury Tales* were immediately popular in England for their portrayal of human nature. The Wife of Bath, however, became very popular while Geoffrey Chaucer was still alive.

Johann Gutenberg developed raised and movable type for printing presses in 1450. In 1476, a man named William Caxton built the first printing press in England. Geoffrey Chaucer was deeply revered and widely read for centuries. Just as Boccaccio had been the greatest influence on Chaucer, so too was Geoffrey Chaucer a tremendous influence on William Shakespeare.

All that is really known of Geoffrey Chaucer's personal life comes from business records of his day. Bonita M. Cox wrote in an essay on Chaucer, "He entertains, he informs, he instructs, and he makes us laugh—but in the final analysis he remains mysterious." [36]

Test Your Knowledge

1 What happened to trigger rebellion in 1395?

  a. The Catholic Church forbade the subject of love to be discussed in poetry.

  b. The Lollards put a list of things they did not like on the door of St. Paul's Cathedral.

  c. The rulers of England required that all peasants contribute part of their pay to the government.

  d. King Richard married a French princess when the queen died.

2 What did Henry of Bolingbroke do to King Richard?

  a. Had him killed

  b. Had him deposed

  c. Had him excommunicated

  d. Had him knighted

3 What was probably the cause of Chaucer's death?

  a. Malaria

  b. Grief

  c. The Black Death

  d. Old age

4 What happened to Chaucer's son Thomas in 1400, the year of Chaucer's death?

  a. He was made sheriff of Oxfordshire.

  b. His wife had a baby.

  c. He got married.

  d. He became the king's butler.

5 Who developed raised and moveable type
for printing presses?
a. Geoffrey Chaucer
b. Giovanni Boccaccio
c. William Caxton
d. Johann Gutenberg

ANSWERS: 1. b; 2. b; 3. c; 4. a; 5. d

1330   Edward III is crowned king of England.

1337   The Hundred Years' War begins.

c. 1340   Geoffrey Chaucer is born.

1346   England wins the Battle of Crecy in France.

1347   The Black Death arrives in Italy.

1348   The Black Death reaches England.

1350   Boccaccio writes *The Decameron.*

1356   England is victorious at Battle of Poitiers in France.

1357   Chaucer becomes a page.

1359–1360   Chaucer goes to war in France.

1360   Chaucer is captured by the French.

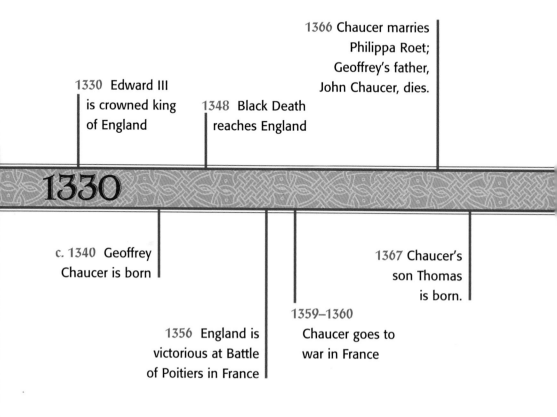

1366 Chaucer marries Philippa Roet; Geoffrey's father, John Chaucer, dies.

1330 Edward III is crowned king of England

1348 Black Death reaches England

1330

c. 1340 Geoffrey Chaucer is born

1367 Chaucer's son Thomas is born.

1356 England is victorious at Battle of Poitiers in France

1359–1360 Chaucer goes to war in France

1361–1362   New outbreak of the Black Death emerges.

1366   Chaucer marries Philippa Roet; Geoffrey's father, John Chaucer, dies.

1367   Chaucer's son Thomas is born.

1368–1372   Chaucer writes *The Book of the Duchess*.

1372   Chaucer travels to Italy for the first time.

1374   Chaucer is appointed as a controller of customs.

1376   The Prince of Wales dies.

1377   King Edward III dies; Richard becomes king.

  The Lollard movement starts under John Wycliff.

1378   Chaucer travels to Italy.

1400 Chaucer and King Richard II die

1368–1372 Chaucer writes *The Book of the Duchess*

1387–1392 Chaucer begins *The Canterbury Tales*

1400

1380 Chaucer's son Lewis is born

1396–1400 Chaucer works on *The Canterbury Tales*

1378–1379 Chaucer writes *The House of Fame*

1378–1379	Chaucer writes *The House of Fame.*
1380	Chaucer's son Lewis is born.
1381	The Peasants' Revolt takes place.
	Chaucer's mother, Agnes Chaucer, dies.
1382	King Richard II marries Anne of Bohemia.
	John Wycliff completes the first translation of the Bible.
1382–1386	Chaucer writes *Troilus and Criseyde.*
1385–1387	Chaucer writes *The Legend of Good Women* and other works.
1385–1389	Chaucer serves as a justice of the peace in Kent.
1386	Chaucer resigns from customs, moves to Kent.
	Chaucer serves in Parliament.
1387–1392	Chaucer begins *The Canterbury Tales.*
1389	Chaucer is appointed as a clerk of the works at Westminster.
1392–1395	Chaucer writes most of *The Canterbury Tales.*
1394	Queen Anne dies.
1396	King Richard II marries Isabella of France.
1396–1400	Chaucer works on *The Canterbury Tales.*
1399	John of Gaunt dies.
	King Richard II is deposed by Henry of Bolingbroke, who becomes King Henry IV.
	Chaucer becomes a tenant at Westminster Abbey.
1400	Chaucer and King Richard II die.

CHAPTER 1
Chaucer the Celebrated Poet

1. Theodore Morrison, *The Portable Chaucer*. New York: The Viking Press, 1949, p. 225.
2. Larry D. Benson, ed. "The Beginnings of Chaucer's Style," in *Geoffrey Chaucer*. Philadelphia: Chelsea House Publishers, 2003, p. 116.

CHAPTER 2
Chaucer the Boy

3. Jeffrey L. Singman and Will McLean, *Daily Life in Chaucer's England*. Westport, CT: Greenwood Press, 1995, pp. 40–41.
4. Marchette Chute, *Geoffrey Chaucer of England*. London: Robert Hale Limited, 1951, p. 92.
5. Ibid., p. 23.
6. Barbara W. Tuchman, *A Distant Mirror: The Calamitous 14th Century*. New York: Ballantine Books, 1978, p. 93.

CHAPTER 3
Chaucer the Young Man

7. Ellyn Sanna, "Biography of Geoffrey Chaucer," in *Geoffrey Chaucer*. Philadelphia: Chelsea House Publishers, 2003, p. 11.
8. Ibid., p. 14.
9. Tuchman, *A Distant Mirror: The Calamitous 14th Century*, pp. 145–146.

10. Sanna, "Biography of Geoffrey Chaucer," p. 13.
11. Ibid, p. 13
12. Tuchman, *A Distant Mirror: The Calamitous 14th Century*, p. 287.

CHAPTER 4
Chaucer the English Poet

13. Singman and McLean, *Daily Life in Chaucer's England*, pp. 52–55.
14. Sanna, "Biography of Geoffrey Chaucer," p. 15.
15. "The Romance of the Rose," The Norton Anthology of English Literature, available online at http://www.wwnorton.com/nael/middleages/topic_1/rose.htm
16. F. N. Robinson, ed., *The Complete Works of Geoffrey Chaucer*. Boston: Houghton Mifflin Company, 1933, p. 316.
17. Benson, "The Beginnings of Chaucer's English Style," p. 98.
18. Tuchman, *A Distant Mirror: The Calamitous 14th Century*, p. 58.

CHAPTER 5
Chaucer in Dual Roles

19. Chute, *Geoffrey Chaucer of England*, p. 107.
20. Ibid., p. 100.
21. Tuchman, *A Distant Mirror: The Calamitous 14th Century*, pp. 374–376.

NOTES

CHAPTER 6
Chaucer in Transition

22. Sanna, "Biography of Geoffrey Chaucer," p. 26.
23. Ibid., pp. 31-32
24. Bonita M. Cox, "Geoffrey Chaucer: "[T]he firste fyndere of our faire language," in *Geoffrey Chaucer*. Philadelphia: Chelsea House Publishers, 2003, pp. 54–58.
25. Chute, *Geoffrey Chaucer of England*, pp. 189–192.
26. Morrison, *The Portable Chaucer*, pp. 373–379.

CHAPTER 7
Chaucer and *The Canterbury Tales*

27. John H. Fisher, "A Language Policy for Lancastrian England," in *Geoffrey Chaucer*. Philadelphia: Chelsea House Publishers, 2003, p. 133.
28. Morrison, *The Portable Chaucer*, p. 87.
29. Cox, "Geoffrey Chaucer: "[T]he first fyndere of our faire language," p. 61.
30. Robert L. James, *On Chaucer's The Canterbury Tales*. Hoboken, NJ: John Wiley & Sons Publishers, 2000, p. 4.
31. Morrison, *The Portable Chaucer*, p. 364.
32. John Brockman, "God (or not), Physics and, of Course, Love: Scientists Take a Leap," *The New York Times,* January 4, 2005, p. D3.

CHAPTER 8
Chaucer and the Theme of Marriage

33. Tuchman, *A Distant Mirror: The Calamitous 14th Century*, pp. 213–218.
34. G.M. Trevelyan, *History of England*. New York: Doubleday Anchor Books, 1952, vol. 1, pp. 342–43.

CHAPTER 9
Chaucer's Final Years

35. Chute, *Geoffrey Chaucer of England*, p. 289.
36. Cox, "Geoffrey Chaucer: [T]he first fyndere of our faire language," p. 45.

BIBLIOGRAPHY

Benson, Larry D., ed. "The Beginnings of Chaucer's Style," in *Geoffrey Chaucer*. Philadelphia: Chelsea House Publishers, 2003.

Brockman, John. "God (or not), Physics and, of Course, Love: Scientists Take a Leap," *The New York Times*. January 4, 2005.

Chute, Marchette. *Geoffrey Chaucer of England*. London: Robert Hale Limited, 1951.

Cox, Bonita M. "Geoffrey Chaucer: "[T]he first fyndere of our faire language" in *Geoffrey Chaucer*. Philadelphia: Chelsea House Publishers, 2003.

Fisher, John H. "A Language Policy for Lancastrian England," in *Geoffrey Chaucer*. Philadelphia: Chelsea House Publishers, 2003.

James, Robert L., Ph.D. *Notes On Chaucer's The Canterbury Tales*. Hoboken, NJ: John Wiley & Sons Publishers, 2000.

Kittredge, George Lyman. "Chaucer's Discussion of Marriage," in *Geoffrey Chaucer*. Philadelphia: Chelsea House Publishers, 2003.

Morrison, Theodore. *The Portable Chaucer*. New York: Viking Press, 1949.

Robinson, F.N., ed. *The Complete Works of Geoffrey Chaucer*. Boston: Houghton Mifflin Company, 1933.

Sanna, Ellyn. "Biography of Geoffrey Chaucer," in *Geoffrey Chaucer*. Philadelphia: Chelsea House Publishers, 2003.

Singman, Jeffrey L., and Will McLean. *Daily Life in Chaucer's England*. Westport, CT: Greenwood Press, 1995.

Tuchman, Barbara W. *A Distant Mirror: The Calamitous 14th Century*. New York: Ballantine Books, 1978.

Benson, Larry D., ed. *The Riverside Chaucer.* Boston: Houghton Mifflin, 1987.

Cooper, Helen. *Oxford Guides to Chaucer: The Canterbury Tales.* New York: Oxford University Press, 1989.

Howard, Donald. *Chaucer: His Life, His Works, His World.* New York: Fawcett Columbine, 1987.

West, Richard. *Chaucer: 1340–1400: The Life and Times of the First English Poet.* New York: Caroll & Graf, 2000.

Websites

Chaucer's Canterbury Tales
http://www.canterburytales.org/canterbury_tales.html

Chaucer's Troilus and Criseyde
http://sunsite.berkeley.edu/OMACL/Troilus/

The Geoffrey Chaucer Homepage
http://www.courses.fas.harvard.edu/~chaucer/

**Medieval Sourcebook: Geoffrey Chaucer
Canterbury Tales: Prologue**
http://www.fordham.edu/halsall/source/CT-prolog-para.html

PICTURE CREDITS

Janet Hubbard-Brown has written numerous books for children and young adults. She is currently writing an adult mystery series set in the wine districts of France with coauthor Astrid Latapie of Paris. She lives in Vermont.